THE BEST DANCE MOVES
IN THE WORLD...EVER!

THE BEST DANCE MOVES IN THE WORLD...EVER!

100 New and Classic Moves and How to Bust Them

by Matt Pagett

CHRONICLE BOOKS

SAN FRANCISCO

Library of Congress Cataloging-in-Publication Data available.

ISBN 978-0-8118-6303-2

Manufactured in China

Conceived, designed and produced by Quid Publishing
Level 4, Sheridan House
114 Western Road
Hove BN3 1DD
www.quidpublishing.com
Designed by rehabdesign™

10 9 8 7 6 5 4 3 2 1

Chronicle Books LLC
680 Second Street
San Francisco, California 94107

www.chroniclebooks.com

adidas is a registered trademark of the adidas Group. Formica is a registered
trademark of Formica Corporation.

None of the performers, songwriters, artists, or copyright holders associated with
the films, television shows, stage shows, and songs mentioned within in any way
sponsor, endorse, or support this book.

Have fun dancing, but please note that:
The author, publisher, and copyright holder assume no responsibility for any
injury, loss, or damage caused or sustained as a consequence of the use and
application of the contents of this book.

Acknowledgments

Thanks (and not just for the dancing) to Alasdair, Em, Jen, Liz, Matt, Mitch, Mon, Ricky, and Sam. Large thanks also to Mike at Rehab, Gabriel for the original idea, and everyone at Quid.

Contents

Introduction

In your hands is a book that has taken centuries to write. It's a book that's constantly being rewritten. It's a book that celebrates the millions of people who have, at one time or another, gotten up off their butts and moved their bodies around— usually in time with a rhythmic beat.

Sow the Seeds

Finger Bopping

Why do we dance? Because we like it? Because it's a release? Because it's a form of creativity? Because we can hang out with our buddies and be a bit stupid? Who knows, and really, who cares? Dance is, and surely that's enough.

Dance is indeed a universal language. It cares not for politics or boundaries, status or wealth, dogma or religion (as Nietzsche once wrote, "I would believe only in a god that knows how to dance"). True, all that crap has attached itself to dance throughout history, probably because the bureaucrats, the stooges, and the bishops have all recognized the fundamental yet simple power held within: the pure power of enjoyable physical activity.

Agadoo

Use this book as a guide to what has been achieved in the last century or so of dance, from Agadoo to Y.M.C.A., from the Chicken Dance through the Chicken Noodle Soup to the Funky Chicken. There's a snake, a monkey, a pony, a worm, and Roger Rabbit; a shuffle from Melbourne, a shake from Harlem, and a walk

like an Egyptian; a toprock and a downrock; jacking, jiving, hitching, and hustling; the Twist, the Stomp, the Mashed Potato too, any old dance that you wanna do. . . . And a fair few new ones too.

Climb the Ladder

The James Brown

for a successful bust. The moves can be roughly divided into various categories, and the index at the back has been organized to help you navigate your way.

Section 1 is an introduction to dance —its history, its recent pioneers, the kinds of music you might dance to, the kinds of clothing you might dance in, and then some general advice.

There are plenty that are missing, and others in here that may well have alternative methods or different names. Some will be familiar to you, some will be overfamiliar, others will be as fresh as an unused dance floor.

The Twist

Stack the Shelves

Then comes section 2: a total of 100 moves for your perusal. Each one is introduced with a bit of history if appropriate, a level of difficulty (none are really THAT hard), and useful tips and suggestions. Then follows a series of either four or eight illustrations (depending on complexity), combined with clear instructions

Step up, step on, groove on. . . .

Section 1
The Basics

"Put Your Glad Rags On . . ."

If you wear something that makes you feel uncomfortable or self-conscious, it'll show in your moves; but if you wear your favorite gear, you'll end up not noticing it, leaving you to get on with getting down. Here are a few wardrobe markers. . . .

If you're putting in some practice at home, it's best to wear loose, comfortable clothing that will allow you to move freely. You're focusing here on how you're dancing, rather than what you're wearing—that comes later. Choose a pair of sneakers, or similarly comfortable shoes, that will give you a bit of a bounce; and for the moves that require fancier footwork, just wear your socks.

Fabric should be light and breathable and allow a full range of unrestricted movements (a sweatsuit or leggings and a T-shirt are ideal). Practice on a hard surface—there aren't many dance floors out there made of carpet—and if there's none around, take a tip from the B-boys and lay down some old cardboard or Formica.

When it comes to going out, your choice of clothes will of course be colored by what kind of event or party it is you're attending. If you're planning on doing any dancing at all, though, you're likely to get hot and sticky. Have a bath

or shower before heading out, and use a deodorant if you think you're going to need one. Go easy on perfumes and aftershaves—not everyone appreciates a cloud of synthetic stink in their face.

Wherever you're going, don't weigh yourself down with unnecessary baggage, clothing, or accessories. Keep things light and you'll appreciate it much more, especially when it comes to going home. However, unless it's really hot outside, take a coat with you—you'll be grateful when you emerge from a sweatbox into the cold night air.

If you're heading to a club, sneakers or similar flat- and soft-bottomed shoes are going to keep your feet most comfortable. You'll likely be standing up most of the time, so it makes sense to minimize any damage. The slight spring they'll put in your step will also be handy when it comes to dancing.

Wearing pants with pockets means that you'll be able to keep your money, keys, and any other essentials close to you without the need for a hefty wallet or purse. That said, you can get small stash bags (particularly for women) that sit over your shoulder and give you minimal hassle.

Dressing for comfort doesn't have to mean that you look like a bag of trash, though. And of course, some clubs positively encourage dressing up, and at these what you wear is as important as the music that's playing and how you're dancing to it. Find out what works best for you, but always keep things on YOUR terms, no one else's.

For a more formal occasion, like a work function or family wedding, you've still got to keep it comfy. Women should avoid stilettos—a kitten heel or wedge will still give you a bit of height without the risk of breaking your ankle. Avoid tight, restrictive skirts, and the larger-busted lady may want to steer clear of anything strapless: put your hands in the air and you may well end up shaking more than you bargained for. A simple wrap or foxy cardigan is a good idea in case you get cold between dances.

For guys, suits are normally easy enough to maneuver in, and are especially handy since you can shed your jacket and tie as the evening warms up. Suit material is generally not that flexible, however, so unless you want to rip a hole in your pants, bear that in mind. Sneakers are pretty much unsuitable; flat shoes instead will allow some pretty impressive footwork.

Some classic accessories you may want to think about wearing or taking with you are:
- a studded belt and spandex pants for a rock concert
- a whistle and smiley-face T-shirt for a rave
- a medallion for a disco
- a baseball cap for a hip-hop night
- leg warmers and fingerless gloves for a 1980s night.

Classic Dance Outfits

Josephine Baker's banana dress (Paris, 1925)

John Travolta's white suit (*Saturday Night Fever* poster, 1977)

Michael Jackson's jacket and white socks ("Thriller" video, 1983)

David Byrne's oversized white jacket (*Stop Making Sense* concert movie, 1984)

Run-D.M.C.'s adidas laceless shell-toes (their whole career)

Madonna's conical bra (Blond Ambition Tour, 1990)

MC Hammer's parachute pants ("U Can't Touch This" video, 1990)

A Concise History of Dance

Dance: a noun, a verb, a way of life. The word itself probably dates back about a thousand years, but people have been rhythmically moving their bodies to a series of beats for an awful lot longer. Since the earliest civilizations, dance has held essential social, ceremonial, and celebratory purposes. Its development is inextricably bound up with that of music, as they both depend on movement and rhythm. Which came first, though, is anyone's guess.

WAY BACK WHEN

They got jiggy with it in ancient India, busted out all over in ancient Egypt (well before the Bangles), and the ancient Greeks believed it had been handed down to mortals by the gods. Not for nothing does Justin Timberlake insist on his entourage praying to Shiva, Hindu god of dance, before every sold-out stadium show. Archeological finds such as statuettes and manuscripts point to the importance of dancing to all sorts of ancient cultures.

THE BIBLE

The most famous dance in the Bible is that performed by Salome, the daughter of Herodias and Herod II, for her stepfather Herod Antipas at his birthday feast. Her moves so enchanted the tetrarch that he offered her whatever she desired. At the suggestion of her mother Herodias, she asked for, and received, the head of John the Baptist, who'd been criticizing her mom's new marriage on the grounds of adultery. Makes a change from winning a silver trophy!

More recently, Andrew Lloyd Webber and Tim Rice gave a new twist to the story of Jesus' last few weeks with the all-singing, all-dancing musical *Jesus Christ Superstar*. Did Jesus really bust a Hustle on his way to the cross?

RENAISSANCE AND LATER

Rufty Tufty, Toss the Duchess, and the Hole in the Wall may sound like low-budget porn flicks, but they're all actually dances from 16th- and 17th-century Europe. From the Renaissance onward, dance developed into many of the more formal styles around today, such as flamenco, ballet, and tango; all from traditions as varied as toffs strutting their way around a ballroom to peasants hitting each other with hog bladders in time with the music. Throughout history, all social strata have embraced the power of dance.

The Waltz

The story of the Waltz serves as a typical example of the development of a formal dance. Performed in couples, it emerged from the ballrooms of 17th-century Austria, though the music, and some of the moves, have roots in earlier Austrian peasant traditions. Lambasted at various points in its history for being lewd and obscene (*The Times* of London, having witnessed it danced at a ball in 1816, felt it "a duty to warn every parent against exposing his daughter to so fatal a contagion"), the Waltz's star continued to rise until, by the early 20th century, all kinds of variations existed. "Waltzing Matilda" is the unofficial anthem of Australia, but has nothing to do with shimmying gowns and orchestras.

THE 20TH CENTURY AND BEYOND

From flappers doing the Charleston with a joy and vigor entirely suited to a post–World War I culture to Missy Elliott getting "hr" freak on for the MTV generation, dance remained at the heart of culture throughout the 20th century. In the early 1900s, rapid developments in travel increased the mobility of the world's population and, as the resulting cultural exchanges escalated, crossover genres soon flourished. Jazz borrowed from African tribal traditions, line dancing took inspiration from the European polka, the mambo spread out from Cuba, and so on. Technological advances have since enabled more recent generations to create new music, with new accompanying moves (witness the growth of hip-hop with breaking, for example).

The rise of the individual in later years, which was arguably ushered in by the snaking hips of a certain Mr. E. Presley, has further set the dance floor free from the tyranny of set dances with rigid moves. Everyone is now free to shake their respective things in whatever way they feel, so long as they're, indeed, shaking. Disco loosened up the collective limbs, and performers such as Michael Jackson, Madonna, and Beyoncé continue to inspire hundreds of bedroom-to-dance-floor moves and routines.

Dance remains a key tool in terms of self-expression and communication, and is no longer confined to performing the right steps in the right order. It's a universal language, a powerful tool, regardless of age, gender, sexuality, race, or religion. . . .

Music: A Bluffer's Guide

Dancing would be virtually impossible without something to dance to. The plethora of sounds available to the modern dancer can be intimidating, particularly to the newcomer. Here then, is a list of the various genres of music one may be expected to groove with, be it at a club, work function, or house party.

POP

Short for "popular," pop music is a many-headed beast with an appeal that reaches across continents and cultures. Pop evades too tight a definition, but can generally be characterized by songs lasting not much more than three to four minutes with a simple melody, rhythm, and structure (such as verse-chorus-verse-chorus-bridge-chorus), and lyrics concerning love, sex, and dancing itself.

Classic pop acts: ABBA, the Beatles, Britney Spears, Duran Duran, Madonna, Elton John.

RnB

RnB has developed into a catch-all term for African-American soul- and funk-inspired pop music, a world away from the phrase's origins when, as a marketing term, "rhythm and blues" described the fusion of 12-bar blues with the boogie-woogie in the 1940s. Nowadays, it covers music with lavish production values, drum machines, maybe a bit of hip-hop thrown in, and smooth vocals.

Classic RnB acts: Usher, Alicia Keys, Mariah Carey, Whitney Houston.

SOUL

Coming out of gospel, jazz, and (original) rhythm and blues traditions of America, soul music hit a peak of popularity in the 1960s. Different areas produced different sounds (for example, compare the Motown sound from Detroit to Memphis' Southern Soul), and it mutated as various other influences crept in. Its main features (if they can be generalized at all) are soaring vocals with raw production including horns, strings, and the odd handclap.

Classic soul acts: Aretha Franklin, Marvin Gaye, Otis Redding, Curtis Mayfield, the Staple Singers.

FUNK

Soul, jazz, and RnB came together to give us funk. Heavily influenced by the Motown sound, the emphasis in funk is on a groove powered by a deep bassline and drumbeats, topped off with electric guitars, keyboards, and horns. Coming alive in the 1960s and 1970s, it was a

huge influence on the birth of disco, and now contemporary hip-hop frequently samples old funk tunes.

Classic funk acts: James Brown, Sly and the Family Stone, George Clinton, Prince, Jamiroquai.

DISCO
In the 1970s, new technologies meant new sounds, and disco was the first genre to really use them, leading to a greater role for the producer. Its roots are in 1960s and 1970s soul and funk. The beat is usually simple (like pop) while the bassline is syncopated (stressing the downbeat, for instance). Lush strings, horns, and electric guitars and pianos complete the sound.

Classic disco acts: The Bee Gees, Donna Summer, Boney M.

HIP-HOP
Percussion breaks in soul, funk, and disco tracks were repeated thanks to the DJ using two turntables, and an MC would then rap over the music. That is how hip-hop music started and essentially how it continues—sampling and rapping. From humble beginnings in block parties in 1970s New York has spread a cultural phenomenon, incorporating art, dance, and the spoken word. Not so much a style as a movement.

Classic hip-hop acts: Kool DJ Herc, Public Enemy, Run-D.M.C., Dr. Dre.

HOUSE
Coming out of Chicago in the early 1980s, house also used soul, funk, and disco—but to very different ends. DJs and producers would

play around with synthesizers, drum machines, sequencers, and samplers to create a wholly manufactured sound, and one dominated by the booming bassline, marking four fast beats to the bar. House made more of an impact in the U.K. in the 1990s, with the government so concerned about illegal raves playing such "repetitive beats" that they were outlawed.

Classic house acts: Frankie Knuckles, Marshall Jefferson, Orbital.

ROCK
Another übergenre, rock has given birth to countless mini-rocks and sub-rocks over the years. General features are vocals, drums, bass, and electric or acoustic guitar—the latter often given a leading role. Other instruments such as keyboards and strings feature too. Rock music evolved out of rock 'n' roll and rockabilly, and continues to mutate into fresh forms.

Classic rock acts: The Rolling Stones, Pink Floyd, Rush, Nirvana, Oasis.

ROCK 'N' ROLL
The term "rock 'n' roll" was originally an African-American slang term for either dancing or sex, so let's keep it clean and stick to the former. Starting in late 1940s America, it combined influences from blues, gospel, country, and jazz to create a startlingly new sound, played on drums, bass, one or two electric guitars, and vocals. Rock 'n' roll went on to influence many later genres, and formed the soundtrack to a time of great social change in the 1950s and 1960s.

Classic rock 'n' roll acts: Elvis Presley, Little Richard, Buddy Holly, Bill Haley.

Pioneers: The Dance Hall of Fame

The dance revolution of the 20th century would not have been possible without a number of key individuals. We salute their influence here.

JOSEPHINE BAKER

Born in 1906, African-American singer and performer Josephine Baker is often considered the original diva. Having moved to France in her early twenties, she helped popularize the Jazz Age styles in Europe as she performed—wearing little more than high heels and a skirt made of bananas. Keeping her company on stage would be her pet cheetah, with a diamond-encrusted collar around its neck. She later became involved in the Resistance movement in wartime France and did much to further the cause of the civil rights movement in her home country. Hemingway called her "sensational" and, as a trailblazer, no one could touch her.

See: The Charleston (pages 168–9), the Shimmy (page 113), the Wing Dance (page 135).

CHUBBY CHECKER

Checker, born Ernest Evans in Philadelphia, struck gold with his 1959 song "The Twist." Incredibly, by today's standards, the song took nearly 14 months of nonstop interviews and touring by the singer before it reached number one. It was the first of many dance crazes to power the rock 'n' roll engine of the late 1950s and 1960s, encouraging young hipsters to break free from all that dancing in couples and get their own groove on instead. Checker went on to have a series of hits with similar songs, each coming with its own dance.

See: The Twist (pages 56–7), the Pony (pages 36–7), the Watusi (page 170).

JAMES BROWN

From the time of his first performances in detention centers when he was still a teenager to his death on Christmas Day in 2006, James Brown did perhaps more than anyone to revolutionize and influence the development of popular music and dance cultures. As a singer, songwriter, bandleader, and producer, much of what is heard today owes some kind of debt to him. Without his frenetic dancing style, characterized by zippy footwork and sweaty acrobatics, dance floors would still be dry.

See: The James Brown (page 42), the Funky Chicken (page 129), the Robot (pages 106–7), the Indian Step (pages 130–1), the Mashed Potato (page 152).

JOHN TRAVOLTA

Having had some mild success acting and singing, it wasn't until he got to dancing in *Saturday Night Fever* in 1977 that the world took notice of John Travolta. Though he was no choreographer, he became the acceptable face of disco, a genre that up until then had pretty much been the reserve of African-American gay guys. The scorching high camp of someone like Sylvester was rejected in favor of this streetwise Italian Stallion, who'd later hit it off on film with Olivia Newton-John and Uma Thurman.

See: Saturday Night Fever (pages 24–5), the Travolta (page 94), Greased Lightnin' (page 158), Pulp Fiction (pages 76–7).

MICHAEL JACKSON

Fame may well have done some mighty strange things with the Prince of Pop's face and brain, but Michael Jackson's influence on dance remains strong. Although his style was hardly new (see James Brown, facing page), he was able to lavish enough money on his promotional videos that the MTV generation were soon eating out of his white-gloved hand, doing their own spins, moonwalks, and zombie dances. Alas, the image on the screen was to grow so monstrous that it would turn around and swallow the poor boy whole, but what moves he left!

See: The Moonwalk (pages 72–3), Thriller (pages 136–7).

BOOGALOO SAM

Whether Boogaloo Sam in mid-1970s California was really the very first to invent "popping" and "booging" remains a hotly debated matter. What is undeniable is the influence he and his band of dancers, the Electric Boogaloos, had on the dance styles of the day and beyond. Jerky, jolting popping and the freer, more fluid booging were their funk styles, which were then fused into the breaking styles of East Coast B-boys and B-girls. Cue the media frenzy. . . .

See: Popping (pages 114–15), the Old Man (pages 166–7), the Armwave (pages 52–3).

Others include:

Malcolm McLaren (punk/hip-hop), Afrika Bambaataa (hip-hop), Madonna (pop), Beyoncé Knowles (pop), Larry Levan (house), Ron Hardy (house), Elvis Presley (rock 'n' roll), among many others.

Tips: Stuff You Should Know

Before you hit the dance floor and start strutting your funky stuff, you should take a few moments to think about the basics.

DO:

✔ Familiarize yourself with music. Have it playing in the house when you're chilling out or doing housework, or listen to a favorite CD instead of watching TV. If there's a radio near you now as you read this, go and put it on. Listen to what's coming out—is it loud or quiet? What instruments are there? What's the rhythm like? You don't even have to be dancing. But the more comfortable you are listening to music, the easier it is to move with it.

✔ Familiarize yourself with your body. Dancing is a physical as well as a mental activity, and if your head is too far apart from the rest of you, you'll feel disconnected, and that's going to show. If need be, go around the house with nothing on. Check yourself out in the mirror. And don't be too hard on yourself if you don't see what you want to see.

✔ When you are first learning a new move, try to take it slowly. Nail the positioning first—where your hands are going, where your feet are meant to be, and so on—and then, once you're more comfortable, you can gradually increase the pace.

✔ Warm up properly. Launching yourself cold into a Six Step (page 124) could lead to torn pants and muscles. Ease yourself in gently.

✔ Feel the rhythm. If you're unsure where the beat is lying, stand still and see if you can lightly tap the beat out with your fingers against your leg. Maybe check out other dancers to see if they've got it. Once you feel it, bring in a foot tap or head nod—the rest should follow in time.

✔ Keep your head up. When you learn new moves, your feet become the most fascinating things ever. Once learned, though, give up the gazing and look around you. You'll feel more confident for it.

✔ Start simple. The mantra "less is more" is a good one to remember. It's much better to be a slightly wary dancer pulling some well-executed smaller moves than an over-confident limb-wielder.

✔ Practice, practice, practice, practice. . . .

DON'T:

✗ Think you can't dance. Start like that and you set yourself up to fail.

✗ Think you're the greatest dancer simply because you know what certain moves involve. You can't call yourself a baker just because you know the ingredients for a loaf of bread. Technique, approach, and self-belief are invisible qualities that will separate the wheat from the chaff.

✗ Take up all the room on the dance floor. Dancing is a social activity, so try to be aware of other people in your vicinity, particularly if going for something like the Boxer (page 145).

✗ Go out with the sole purpose of getting lucky. You'll end up looking and feeling horribly desperate.

✗ Get too drunk. While liquor can certainly help loosen up any fears or awkwardness, too much will do you no favors.

✗ Force non-dancers to dance. There's no worse encouragement than someone bullying you to get on the dance floor.

Using This Book

- Not all the instructions are designed to be followed strictly in order. Feel free to change them around once you know what they're about.
- For quite a lot of the moves, whether you start on your left or right is unimportant. Again, go with whichever is comfortable.
- Most of the time, the focus is on the feet and the hands. Once you know the basics, though, you can fancy up the moves with handclaps, finger clicks, mischievous winks, swaying hips, dipping shoulders, and so on.
- The moves featured here are designed to give you a brief idea of what delights reside inside the diverse world of dance. Use them as a starting point from which your own moves can emerge.

Relax, focus, and enjoy yourself. . . .

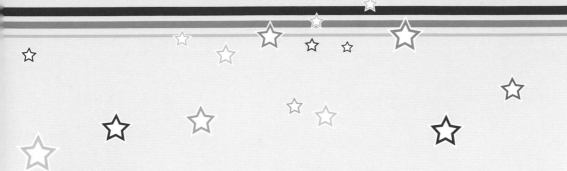

Section 2
The Moves

Classic Moves

Saturday Night Fever

INSPIRATION

1977 saw the release of the most influential, most popular dance-related movie of all time. Saturday Night Fever tells the story of Tony Manero, played by John Travolta, who seeks refuge from his dead-end job and spirit-crushing home life on the dance floor of his local Brooklyn discotheque. Once the beat kicks in, Tony is transformed from an everyday no-hoper to a hotter-than-butter disco super-stud with moves that apparently cannot fail to impress.

LEVEL

Intermediate.

THE SONG

The film's soundtrack was partly composed and recorded by the Bee Gees and helped popularize the disco subculture to a much wider mainstream audience, reviving the group's career in the process. "You Should Be Dancing" is the particular track used for the main dance scene in the film. Bored with

seeing another female devotee spin drearily around in front of him like an old chunk of lamb on a spit, Manero tells himself and her to "forget this," puffs his chest up and out, and struts around the dance floor in time with the bass, parting the assorted hordes like a modern-day Moses. It's Tony time. . . .

POSITIONING

This move can be busted either standing up or, for the more supple, down on one knee.

SUGGESTED PROPS

Flashing underlit dance floor, open shirt, medallion, adoring audience.

NOTES TO DANCERS

There is a fine line between looking like Tony Manero and looking like someone who should sit down and stop dancing. One of the first rules of dancing: know your limits. The following moves are only selected highlights from Travolta's main solo routine.

STEP 1
Rotate your hips and shoulders as you clear the floor with a brisk, slinky walk.

STEP 2
Place your right foot straight ahead, the left foot to the side. Sweep your right arm 180 degrees out in front of you. Thrust your hips.

STEP 3
Right foot out then in, left foot out then in. Repeat for eight on the beat.

STEP 4
Kick your right foot out on the first beat, then bend your knees on the second. Repeat for each 90-degree turn.

STEP 5
Stag jump (split your legs with your front knee bent) through 360 degrees, and land on the floor, with your left leg out and your right tucked under your butt.

STEP 6
Up on your feet, cross both arms. Bend then straighten your legs, propelling your whole body forward.

STEP 7
Jump and stretch your arms and legs so they're parallel with your body (think kids from Fame).

STEP 8
The iconic Travolta (see page 94). Point your right arm above your head, then reach down to the bottom left. Repeat if desired.

The Ass Shaker

INSPIRATION
They're everywhere—on billboards, TV, phones, and computer screens: vixens of the new pop scene rotating their butts up and down, around and around at quite a speed with an impressive dedication. Followers of Beyoncé, Shakira, et al., step forward, shake your tail feathers, and heed the booty call.

LEVEL
Basic. If your ass is too flabby, this move can be practiced (in private) to firm up your glutes before any public performance.

HEALTH WARNING
Too much posterior vibration can cause involuntary muscle spasms, cramps, and even chafing.

SUITABLE MUSIC
Dancehall, RnB, "I See You Baby" by Groove Armada ft. Gram'ma Funk.

STEP 1
Stand with your feet roughly 12 in. (30 cm.) apart, and stick out your ass.

STEP 2
Clench your butt cheeks together, slightly bend your knees, and gyrate your hips in time with the music.

STEP 3
Raise your arms as you continue your actions.

STEP 4
Add some flavor to the routine by jumping around, shaking in various directions.

Finger Bopping

INSPIRATION

For most people, the pleasure of dance lies in full bodily movement in time to a series of rhythmic beats. But for those without the necessary quota of energy, what gives? Finger Bopping is incredibly simple, and suitable for flexible finger fanatics the whole world over. It also promotes manual dexterity (useful in societies dominated by the keyboard).

𝒯op 𝒯ip

For full-body dancers, finger bopping can be inserted into a more full-fledged routine. This will allow movers and shakers to get their breath back and prepare for the next stage.

LEVEL
Ultra basic.

SUITABLE MUSIC
Just about any.

STEP 1
You don't strictly need to be standing up for this one. Raise one hand and extend your index finger.

STEP 2
Bring it back in. . .

STEP 3
. . . then point outward with the same finger. . .

STEP 4
. . . then bring it back in. Incorporate other moves with other fingers, including wagging, clapping, and clicking.

Melbourne Shuffle

INSPIRATION
The Shuffle emerged in the mid-1990s as part of the rave scene. High-octane music and lighting; cavernous spaces filled with thousands of pulsing, sweaty bodies—take your grandma and you may be bringing her out in a box. The dance itself echoes certain breakdance moves, and is an Australian take on the house and techno traditions of the United States and Europe. The emphasis is on gliding effortlessly around the dance floor; your arms can do whatever they want.

LEVEL
Intermediate.

SUITABLE MUSIC
Techno, trance, psytrance, breakbeat, and drum 'n' bass, among others.

POSITIONING
This move can be busted either standing up or, for the more supple, down on one knee.

STEP 1
Put one foot slightly in front of the other, forming a "T."

STEP 2
Rotate your front foot about 60 degrees counterclockwise on its heel, lifting the back foot up at the same time.

Top Tip
Dusting the floor with talcum powder before practice will help your feet glide more easily, as will non-grip soles.

Note
The steps here are just a basic introduction to the Melbourne Shuffle. True to the spirit of the music, dancers are encouraged to move in whatever way they feel.

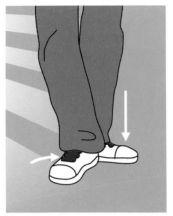

STEP 3

Rotate back to your original position using the ball of your front foot, putting your back foot back on the floor at the same time.

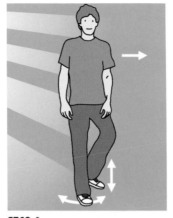

STEP 4

You should aim to move yourself along in a sideways direction with this step.

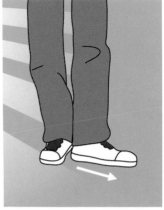

STEP 5

Swap your feet over so the back is now at the front and repeat the move.

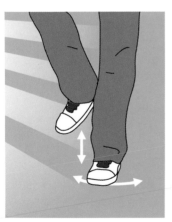

STEP 6

Your back foot goes up and down, your front goes side to side, unless you want to change feet when...

STEP 7

... the back foot comes forward to "take over." Your front foot now takes on the back role.

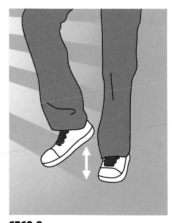

STEP 8

Once you get the hang of it, the back foot can loosen up a bit. Just practice slowly at first, and the rest will soon follow.

The Swim

INSPIRATION

Swimming, so the experts say, is very good for us. It works on our inner organs, improves muscle and skin tone, and promotes a general sense of well-being. If, however, you're scared of the water or don't look great in chlorine-resistant nylon, you may want to incorporate a few of these moves into your next dance floor foray.

LEVEL

Basic.

SUITABLE MUSIC

Anything by Wet Wet Wet, or perhaps a tune from Justin Timber . . . lake.

STEP 1
Stand upright, shoulders back, and move your feet in time with the music.

STEP 2
The breaststroke: bring both arms up to shoulder level, then swing out (ensure there's enough space around you).

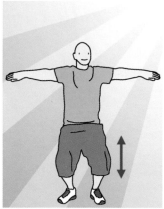

STEP 3
Bend your legs as you bring your arms back to the starting position. Repeat if desired.

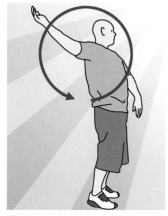

STEP 4
The backstroke: rotate your right arm backward through 360 degrees. . .

STEP 5
. . . then rotate your left arm backward through 360 degrees.

STEP 6
Front crawl: alternately bring each arm over your head and out in front of you.

STEP 7
The dive: pinch your nose and move down to the floor, swaying your body from right to left.

STEP 8
On the way down, raise your free arm over your head and sway that in time.

Sow the Seeds

INSPIRATION
This move may very well have its roots in rural traditions. In fact, fertility dances often formed part of a town or village's celebrations at significant parts of the year, such as harvest, and moves essential for a bountiful crop would be mimed out and incorporated into a larger musical display. By Sowing the Seeds in your local club, therefore, you are keeping the past alive! Well done.

LEVEL
Basic.

ALTERNATIVELY. . .
The action is close to that of dealing a pack of cards. Imagine you are now a croupier, dealing your invisible deck in a glitzy casino.

SUITABLE MUSIC
Something with that arable vibe, like tunes by Wheatus or even Lil' "Barley" Mo.

STEP 1
Standing up, sway in time with the music.

STEP 2
Gracefully reach toward your left armpit with your right arm. . .

STEP 3
. . . then cast your imaginary seeds across the floor in front of you.

STEP 4
Speed up your actions, alternate hands, throw seeds behind you, and distribute freely to add vivacity to your moves.

The Cabbage Patch

INSPIRATION

As much a part of the 1980s as big hair and Back to the Future, the Cabbage Patch was first introduced by the Gucci Crew II in 1987 with the cleverly titled song "The Cabbage Patch." Some American footballers popularized it by incorporating the moves into touchdown celebrations.

LEVEL

Basic.

FACT

Over recent years, it has become more and more popular for sportsmen and -women to celebrate a fine piece of play with their own signature dance move. If the move is performed badly, however, the losing side can console themselves with the fact that the victors are clearly embarrassing themselves. See also the Ickey Shuffle on page 141.

STEP 1
Standing up, extend both arms out in front of you, with one arm across your body to meet the other slightly to one side.

STEP 2
Rotate both arms around in a horizontal circle.

STEP 3
For extra effect, shift your weight from one leg to the other as you complete the circle.

STEP 4
The Cabbage Patch can be performed in both clockwise and counterclockwise directions.

Classic Moves

Agadoo

INSPIRATION

The "novelty song" is one of many curious strands that run through the warp and weft of modern popular music, and "Agadoo" is a classic of the genre. A nursery-rhyme-like tune populated with nonsensical lyrics, it spent many, many weeks in the U.K. charts in the 1980s and took a hold on the public imagination. Play it at any function even now and not even the most studiously cool dancer will be able to resist the call of the "doo" to the dance floor.

LEVEL
Basic.

THE SONG

"Agadoo" was originally a European hit in the 1970s, and a dance routine was made up to go with it by bar staff in a nightclub in northern England. When the group Black Lace performed at the same club in 1981, they learned the dance and covered the song themselves. Three years later, "Agadoo" reached number two in the charts, and the dance was immortalized in a video featuring dancing pineapples and waiters with glacé cherries for heads.

SUGGESTED PROPS
Cocktail shakers, Wayfarer shades, coconuts.

Note

The moves here are only prescribed for the chorus—the rest is up to you.

STEP 1
Point both hands out three times on the "...doo-doo-doo."

STEP 2
Push with both arms out twice (this symbolizes pushing a pineapple, of course).

STEP 3
Link hands and sway them side to side as if you're shaking a tree.

STEP 4
Repeat Steps 1 and 2 for another round of "Agadoo-doo-doo, Push pineapple..."

STEP 5
Quickly rotate your hands around as the band sings "Grind coffee."

STEP 6
Then, following the words of the song, stretch your left arm out to the left, then your right arm out to the right...

STEP 7
...then stretch both arms above, quickly followed by bringing them both back down to your knees.

STEP 8
Finish the display off with some rhythmic clapping, smiles to your fellow dancers, and the loss of any self-consciousness you may have been experiencing.

The Pony

INSPIRATION

"It's Pony time! Get up!"
You'll be cantering crazy
after five minutes of this
one. It's really pretty silly
—you literally impersonate
a horse. The daddy of the
Twist (pages 56–7), Chubby
Checker, released "Pony
Time" as a single in 1961,
and so followed the dance
to go with it. You're in a
stable, with a nosebag
strapped round your ears.
The rhythm is 1+2, 3+4.

LEVEL
Basic.

SUITABLE CLOTHING
Saddle, bit between teeth,
horseshoes.

STEP 1
Hop onto your right leg for
one beat, with your left foot
dangling in the air.

STEP 2
Then hop onto the ball of
your left foot for another beat.

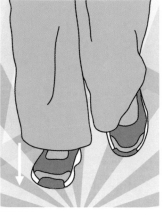

STEP 3
Another step onto your flat right foot and hold for two beats this time.

STEP 4
Now to the other side: jump onto your left foot for a beat...

STEP 5
... then a light hop onto the ball of your right foot...

STEP 6
... then a jump back onto your flat left foot for two beats. And so it goes on. ...

STEP 7
Keep your elbows bent and at your sides, swaying back and forth...

STEP 8
... and throwing in a few lean-ins and lean-outs won't go amiss, either.

Mr./Ms. Distinguished

INSPIRATION
Cut a dash on the dance floor with this simple step. Essentially, all you're doing is brushing your shoulders off, but place the move in the middle of a bigger routine and it allows you a bit of a breather. It also lets your audience know that you are a hygienic dancer about to embark on the next phase of your repertoire.

LEVEL
Basic.

STEP 1
Stand upright with your arms down by your sides.

STEP 2
Turn your head and look at your left shoulder. You can affect a look of mock-disdain if you prefer.

STEP 3
Brush the (hopefully) imaginary dirt or dandruff off your shoulders in time with the music, using your right hand.

STEP 4
Repeat Steps 2 and 3 on your right shoulder. Embellish the move with swaying hips.

The Hitch Hike

INSPIRATION

This is an easy, fun move, particularly useful if you're in need of a lift home. The move was one of many that accompanied the huge explosion in pop music in the early 1960s. The Hitch itself was a craze started by Marvin Gaye's 1962 tune "Hitch Hike" and continued in popularity right though the decade and beyond.

LEVEL

Basic.

STEP 1
With your feet locked to the floor, point your right thumb over your right shoulder for a count of three...

STEP 2
...then clap once.

Note

The featured move here is the classic Motown version, but once you've got your basic thumb movement going (which won't take long), there are loads of variations to play around with. You may want to include the Shimmy (page 113) for a bit of extra oomph.

STEP 3
Same again, but this time with your left thumb—over your left shoulder for three...

STEP 4
...and back for another clap.

Air Guitar

INSPIRATION
Long the preserve of frustrated men of a certain age, who long ago swapped ambitions of becoming a god with a guitar for a career in insurance, these moves are wholly inspired by the monsters of rock— Deep Purple, Motörhead, Iron Maiden, Rush, and so on. Think spandex, think hair, think stadiums, think METAL.

LEVEL
Intermediate.

SUITABLE MUSIC
Anything with a heavy element of guitar playing.

SUGGESTED PROPS
Perm, anything big and long—such as a pool cue.

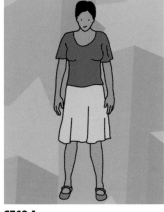

STEP 1
Stand with your legs about 12 in. (30 cm.) apart, body relaxed and head down low (as if weighed down by a large perm).

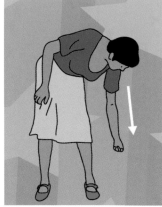

STEP 2
Reach down to your left and plug the imaginary cord from your imaginary guitar into the imaginary amplifier next to your foot.

Note
Aside from the obvious air-guitar playing, the addition of some pre-performance moves will accentuate your aura of authenticity.

STEP 3

Again reach down and twiddle with some imaginary knobs on both the guitar and the amplifier.

STEP 4

When you and the music are ready, strike your first string(s). Make it as dramatic as you wish.

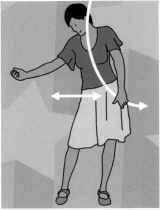

STEP 5

Continue playing, moving your hips, and so on.

STEP 6

Additional singing or lip-synching will impress your audience, and heighten your connection to the music that is being played.

STEP 7

Stunts (such as jumping), exaggerated movements (for example, hip gyrations), and the classic headbang will make your routine unique.

STEP 8

Once finished, stand with your arms aloft as you soak up the crowd's rapturous applause.

The James Brown

INSPIRATION
The Godfather of Soul, the Hardest-Working Man in Showbiz, and Master of the Good Foot, James Brown was a true original. Seeing him live could be a near-religious experience, such was the man's power, vitality, and general funkadelabilicity. He influenced the development of both dance and music to an unsurpassed extent, and his moves would be enough to fill an entire book on its own. This is one of them.

LEVEL
Intermediate.

SUITABLE MUSIC
Funk, soul, hip-hop.

HEALTH WARNING
This move may look scary, but really isn't that bad. It's not for the arthritic, however.

STEP 1
Stand on your left leg and bend your right knee so your foot rests just on the other side of your left knee.

STEP 2
Gently bend your left knee so your whole body is lowered. Stop when the ball of your right foot hits the floor.

STEP 3
Your feet should be crossed, so that as you push up with your legs...

STEP 4
...your whole body turns 360 degrees as you come up.

The Rapper

INSPIRATION

Emerging out of traditions as diverse as African tribal chanting, Jamaican dancehall, disco, and funk (with a dash of Muhammad Ali thrown in), rap's birth and development was inextricably linked to that of hip-hop. Boys and girls from the inner city found new voices and new expressions, and though it looks very different from when it was all starting out in the late 1970s, the rap story continues to flourish.

LEVEL

Basic.

SUGGESTED CLOTHING

Gold chain, sneakers, pants with one leg rolled up to the calf, baseball cap (back to front is an option), huge clock around your neck (à la Flavor Flav), and so on. . . .

STEP 1

Stand with your feet a fair way apart and nod your head and cross your arms as if hugging your favorite teddy bear in the whole wide world.

STEP 2

Mime along with the vocals. Disguise the fact that you may not know the words by holding an imaginary microphone close to your mouth.

STEP 3

Hand gestures are vital: extending your arms in front of you is just one of many possibilities.

STEP 4

Grab your crotch.

The Roger Rabbit

INSPIRATION

The floppy legs of Roger Rabbit are honored with this move, dating from around the time of the film's release, 1988. Often grouped together with what has become known as "breakdancing," it grew out of street dancing traditions in New York, Los Angeles, and other American cities.

LEVEL

Intermediate.

SUITABLE MUSIC

Surely it has to be Jive Bunny and the Mastermixers.

Note

The Roger Rabbit is very close to the Running Man on pages 48–9, but your steps here are coming up from the back rather than down from the front.

STEP 1
Stand with your legs close together, then slide your right foot out to the side, around and up behind your left foot.

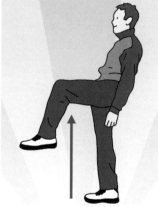

STEP 2
As soon as you feel your right foot hitting the left, bring your left knee up to chest height.

STEP 3
Then lower your left knee, slide your left foot back around to just behind your right foot.

STEP 4
Whenever your knee, left or right, is raised, bring your chest in slightly and bring up your arms.

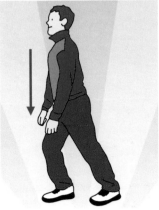

STEP 5
And when both feet are on the floor, your chest should be slightly out and your arms down.

STEP 6
You can also remain lifting and raising the same knee...

STEP 7
...keeping your back foot behind it, swapping the weight from one to the other.

STEP 8
Keep the arms and chest connected to the movements down below.

Classic Moves

Oops Upside Your Head

INSPIRATION

A popular dance at any family party where there is a lot of liquor flowing. As many people as possible sit in a line, one behind the other, and perform these incredibly simple moves to the Gap Band's 1979 funk classic "I Don't Believe You Want to Get Up and Dance (Oops Upside Your Head)," in a kind of rowboat formation.

LEVEL
Basic.

HEALTH WARNING
Because this dance is performed on the floor, anyone with a bad back should avoid participation. Also, watch what you sit in!

THE SONG
The Gap Band formed in Tulsa, Oklahoma, around three core members, brothers Charlie, Robert, and Ronnie Wilson. Their music contained none of the social or political messages found in other funk forms—their priority was always about the music, the dance, and the party. This track was one of the band's earliest releases, and was followed by other notable successes well into the 1980s.

FANCY THAT
"Oops Upside Your Head" has since passed into modern urban parlance. To go oops upside someone's head is to give the back of said head a bit of a slap.

STEP 1

Two or more people should sit behind one another, each with their legs on either side of the person in front.

STEP 2

Clap on the beat, then raise your right arm.

STEP 3

Then clap on the beat, then raise your left arm. Repeat these two steps for a count of eight.

STEP 4

Lean forward for a count of two...

STEP 5

...then lean back for another count of two. Repeat these two steps for a count of eight.

STEP 6

Lean over to your right-hand side with your right arm extended to the floor for a count of two.

STEP 7

Lean to your left side, extending your left arm for a count of two. Again, repeat these two steps for a count of eight.

STEP 8

Repeat Steps 2–7 until the music finishes or inertia kicks in, whichever comes first.

The Running Man
(a.k.a. The Vanilla Ice)

INSPIRATION
Alternatively known as the Vanilla Ice, this move also featured heavily in videos by MC Hammer (see page 104). The Running Man is very close to the Roger Rabbit (pages 44–5) and emerged from the same city streets around the same time (the late 1980s). The essential idea is to look like you're running when in fact you are staying still, thus illustrating the power of illusion. It became such a staple of dance music culture in its time, and people now fondly look back on the time when their joints were supple enough to do the Running Man.

LEVEL
Intermediate.

SUITABLE MUSIC
"Da Doo Run Run" by the Crystals, "Keep on Running" by the Spencer Davis Group, and anything up-tempo by Run-D.M.C.

STEP 1
Raise your right knee up to waist height.

STEP 2
As you take it back down, slide your left foot along the floor behind you.

Top Tip
As with many similar foot-sliding moves, practice on a smooth floor with low-grip shoes or socks.

STEP 3
Then bring your left knee up to waist height...

STEP 4
...and as you bring it down, slide your right foot backward.

STEP 5
Keep practicing until you get a smooth motion going.

STEP 6
Emphasize the movement by bringing your arms up...

STEP 7
...and down in time with the steps.

STEP 8
Spice up the move with some on-the-spot swivels through 180 degrees, then continue, facing the opposite direction.

Jacking

INSPIRATION

"In the beginning there was Jack, and Jack had a groove, and from this groove came the groove of all grooves." Yes indeed, the early house scene, which nudged into existence on the American East Coast in the mid-1980s, saw the development of new ways of thinking about music. DJs and electronic equipment, as opposed to musicians and instruments, came to the fore, and the people dancing started to Jack their bodies like no one had done before.

LEVEL

Basic.

HOUSE MUSIC PIONEERS

Marshall Jefferson, Ron Hardy, Larry Levan, Frankie Knuckles, Larry Heard, DJ Pierre.

SUITABLE MUSIC

"Jack to the Sound of the Underground" by Hithouse.

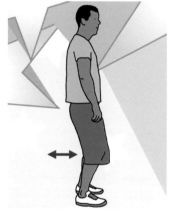

STEP 1
Stand with your feet about 12 in. (30 cm.) apart, and slightly bend then straighten your knees...

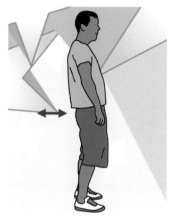

STEP 2
... quickly followed by a slight thrust in your hips.

𝒩ote

These moves are based on the idea of a wave rippling through your body in time with the music. These aren't strictly prescribed, and the ethos of house music is to do what you want, how you want, when you want.

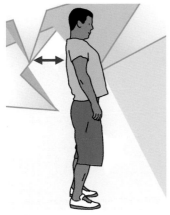

STEP 3

Then bring your chest out, followed by your shoulders, maintaining a smooth rocking motion throughout.

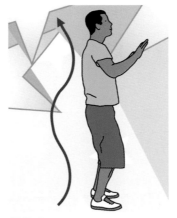

STEP 4

Keep practicing so your body comes to ripple in time with each beat. Incorporate foot and arm gestures once you're feeling confident.

STEP 5

Another form of jacking: hold onto something—a rail, or a chair, for example (not another person, though).

STEP 6

Start to rock your hips back and forth...

STEP 7

...and feel the movement lift through your body up to your shoulders. Keep your feet stationary.

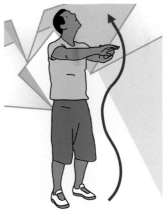

STEP 8

Shake your head as you continue working your whole body, all in time with the music.

The Armwave

INSPIRATION

Another classic B-boy move dating back from the early 1980s, coming from the same roots as the Old Man (pages 166–7), Popping (pages 114–15), and the Robot (pages 106–7)—among others. The general idea here is to give the impression that a wave is traveling through your arms. Once you're well versed in the art, you may want to progress to feeling waves through your chest, legs, even your whole body.

LEVEL

Basic.

SUITABLE MUSIC

Hip-hop, electro, funk.

STEP 1
Stand with your arms straight out at each side, parallel to the floor.

STEP 2
Bend your right wrist so the fingers point down.

Note

The key to a successful Armwave is keeping your body motionless apart from each sequential movement. The elbows can be tricky, but practicing in front of a mirror should sort them out. The steps here are exaggerated, but subtler Armwave is a mark of refinement.

STEP 3
Now bend your elbow up and bring it up...

STEP 4
...then push your whole arm up at the right shoulder.

STEP 5
Raise your left shoulder as you drop the right shoulder...

STEP 6
...then drop your left shoulder as the left elbow comes up. Your hand should be flat and pointing left.

STEP 7
Bring your wrist up so your arm is fully extended, apart from your fingers, which are now pointing down...

STEP 8
...until you bring your fingers up so they're lying flat again.

The V-Sign

INSPIRATION
This is a slinky move, evocative of the 1950s, which somehow hints at disguise and seduction, when done correctly—perfect when dancing with a prospective partner. It was used to good effect in the Jack Rabbit Slim's dance sequence in **Pulp Fiction** *(featured on pages 76–7).*

LEVEL
Basic.

STEP 1
Make a "V" with the index and middle fingers of your right hand and bring it up to eye level, palm out.

STEP 2
Move your hand in front of you from left to right.

STEP 3
Repeat on the left side—shimmy a "V" of your left fingers...

STEP 4
... across from right to left. Repeat as desired.

Big Fish, Little Fish, Cardboard Box

INSPIRATION
A slinky sequence that started out as a parody of the kind of moves busted by early morning ravers at the height of the first acid house parties in 1980s Britain. It has now filtered through popular culture and is now taught to seven-year-old kids at vacation camps. How times change!

LEVEL
Basic.

SUGGESTED MUSIC
Anything with a repetitive beat.

STEP 1
Stand with your hands out in front of you, a fair distance from one another (as if measuring a big fish).

STEP 2
Shrink the size of the imaginary fish on the next beat.

STEP 3
On the next beat, mime a box by switching your hands so they are one above the other...

STEP 4
...then complete the box on the next beat by switching your hands back to mime its sides. Continue in this vein ad infinitum.

Classic Moves

The Twist

INSPIRATION

The early 1960s saw, for the first time, the introduction of dances that could be performed by folks on their own—none of that picking up girls or twirling under boys' arms. Here were new sets of moves that you could bust solo—a phenomenon entirely suited to an age of increasing individualism and sexual liberation. And the Twist was without doubt the most popular.

LEVEL

Basic. The Twist consists of very simple moves that even those without a great sense of rhythm can get away with.

THE SONG

Ernest Evans was a chicken plucker and amateur song style impersonator from Pennsylvania who shot to fame in 1960 when he appeared on the TV show *American Bandstand*, singing Hank Ballard's B-side "The Twist." Evans was urged to change his name to something along the lines of Fats Domino; so "Fats" became "Chubby" and "Domino" became "Checker" and whaddaya know, Chubby Checker had arrived. He eventually recorded versions in French, German, and Italian, ensuring the song's worldwide appeal.

OTHER NOTABLE TWISTS

Later songs such as "Twistin' the Night Away" by Sam Cooke and "Twist and Shout" by the Beatles continued the dance's appeal. In 1987, a new version of the original recorded with rap trio the Fat Boys saw Checker back in the charts (and doubtless did his bank balance no harm, either).

STEP 1

Stand with your legs about 12 in. (30 cm.) apart, then start to twist clockwise on the ball of each foot...

STEP 2

... then twist back counterclockwise. Keep this twisting action going, as if you were perpetually stubbing out a cigarette.

STEP 3

At the same time, keep your elbows in toward your chest and raise your hands up in front of you...

STEP 4

... then move them from side to side, like you're drying your back with a towel. Keep twisting on the balls of your feet.

STEP 5

That's the basic Twist. Add some variation by leaning backward...

STEP 6

... and forward...

STEP 7

... and by moving upward...

STEP 8

... and downward.

The Hustle

INSPIRATION

There's a whole other book's worth in the fine art of line dancing, but the Hustle has worked its way into this one because it can be incorporated into 1970s-style routines and parties: you don't need a check shirt and mustache to bust this one. It was originally danced to the pretty 1975 classic of the same name by Van McCoy, a song that sounds like a couple of chirping birds tweeting over a funky bassline.

LEVEL

Basic, though you do need to concentrate.

OTHER HUSTLES

"Hustle" is a term applied to a number of different other dances. The version for partners takes elements of salsa and swing dancing and is usually known as the New York Hustle or Latin Hustle, while another line dance form is known as the L.A. Bus Stop Hustle.

SUITABLE MUSIC

Disco.

STEP 1
Step backward for a count of four.

STEP 2
Step forward for another count of four.

STEP 3
Turn around to the right (a move known as a Rolling Grapevine—see page 70) for four then clap.

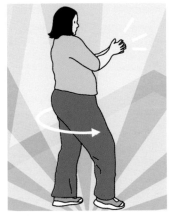

STEP 4
Rolling Grapevine to the left for another four, clapping again on the fourth beat.

STEP 5
Travolta (see page 94) for eight—don't forget to work your hips!

STEP 6
Then an Eggbeater (page 87) for two. . .

STEP 7
. . . a Funky Chicken (page 129) for another two. . .

STEP 8
. . . then step forward, then back, then to the side and a quarter-turn left—each of these on single beats. Then take it from the top!

The Sprinkler

INSPIRATION
Roll out those lazy, hazy, crazy days of summer by busting this sun-beating move. Proving that inspiration can be found in the simplest, weirdest little thing, the Sprinkler is based on a certain type of lawn irrigation system. It's been knocking around since the 1980s and is sure to refresh even the most arid of dance floors.

LEVEL
Intermediate.

SUITABLE MUSIC
Handel's "Water Music," "Raindrops Keep Falling on My Head," "It's Raining Men," "A Hard Spray's Night," and so on. . . .

POSITIONING
This move can be busted either standing up or, for the more supple, down on one knee.

Tip

Why not incorporate this into a routine featuring other garden-based moves (such as the Lawnmower on page 71)? It's particularly suitable if you're trying hard to impress a horticulturalist or flower arranger.

STEP 1
Hold your left arm straight out in front of you. Ball your hand into a fist.

STEP 2
Bring your right fist up to your right ear, with the elbow pointing forward.

STEP 3
In time with the beat, bring your right elbow and your left forearm together and back out again.

STEP 4
Repeat three times while rotating your body 90 degrees to the left, then return to your starting position.

The Say-What?!
(a.k.a. The Double Take)

INSPIRATION
Someone (a family member, a colleague, or a friend) utters something so devastating, catty, or stupid that your head goes into an involuntary spasm of incredulity. Also applies to the disbelieving reaction of seeing someone naked out of the corner of one's eye in a public place.

LEVEL
Basic. This move is ideal for the beginner who may be too scared to even stand up on the dance floor, because it can be performed from the sidelines until their confidence has risen. Hence this move is also good if you're too tired to stay on the dance floor, but still want to bust some moves.

HEALTH WARNING
Sudden jerking of the head can trap nerves, or worse. You should be careful at all times, and definitely don't try it with a sore neck.

SUITABLE MUSIC
Light pop, or anything with a strong beat.

STEP 1
Sitting or standing straight, ensure your head and neck are fully relaxed. Some gentle limbering up is advisable.

STEP 2
On the beat, turn your head to the left.

STEP 3
Immediately start to turn the head to the right.

STEP 4
In time for the next beat, turn back to the left. Additional dramatic effect can be gained by glaring. Repeat process, but this time turning to the right.

The Madison

INSPIRATION

Another routine that helped light the fire of early rock 'n' roll in the late 1950s and 1960s. It's quite a genteel move, focusing solely on the feet, though there are jazzier figures that dancers were expected to perform when called upon to do so. A fine example of the full Madison roll can be seen in John Waters' 1988 film Hairspray.

LEVEL
Basic.

SUITABLE MUSIC
Various Madison-themed tunes were recorded and performed by people like the Ray Bryant Combo, the Tunetoppers, and Count Basie, but really the steps are neat enough to grace any kind of sound.

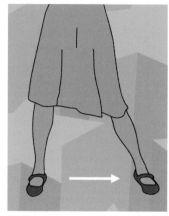

STEP 1
Step your left foot out once to the left.

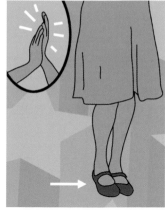

STEP 2
Bring your right foot against it (keep your weight on the left) and clap as you do.

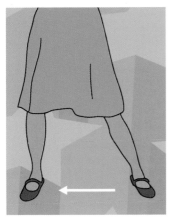

STEP 3
Step back on your right foot to where you were.

STEP 4
Cross your left foot in front of your right (where your weight now is) for a beat.

STEP 5
Uncross for another beat.

STEP 6
Cross back for another. . .

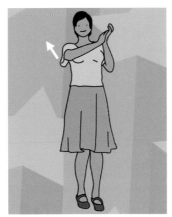

STEP 7
. . . and start all over again. Lean-ins and lean-outs will add a little sparkle. . .

STEP 8
. . . as will shoulder shimmies.

The Snake

INSPIRATION
The Snake has nothing to do with crawling on your belly like a serpent, and everything to do with loosening up your body so that when you shift from side to side the lines you make are like those of a curving boa constrictor. It's one of a slew of moves that came up from the streets in 1980s America.

LEVEL
Intermediate.

ALTERNATIVELY. . .
Another Snake is where a group of assorted B-boys and B-girls hold hands in a circle and perform a multi-person Armwave (see pages 52–3). This one here is the other version.

STEP 1
Stand with your arms bent, hands out in front of you, and step once out to the right. At the same time. . .

STEP 2
. . . move your head to the right, but make it slinky: bend your head slightly toward your shoulder, then straighten it up.

STEP 3

As your head straightens, create a roll through your body by lifting and raising your chest swiftly, followed by a slight roll of your hips...

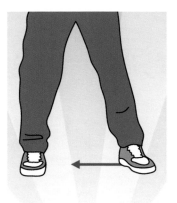

STEP 4

... while at the same time sliding your left foot across to meet your right. This should be the last action, and is what creates the snake-like flow.

STEP 5

As your foot slides, slide your hands across.

STEP 6

Now back—move your head to the left as you step out once to the left...

STEP 7

... rolling your body down (don't over-exaggerate the roll, though) until your right foot slides to the left.

STEP 8

Slide your two hands across to the left at the same time as your foot slides.

Classic Moves

Vogue

INSPIRATION

With its roots in 1930s "Performance" traditions in Harlem, Voguing became a vehicle for expression for young, gay, predominantly African-American and Latino drag kings and queens—and it remains popular today, though not as much as when Madonna hitched a ride on its coattails and took "Vogue" to number one in 1990. The moves featured here are some of those popularized by her "Vogue" video. Pull any of them at the exclusive balls held by the professionals, and you're likely to be skinned alive under a screaming mass of fake fur and fingernails.

LEVEL

Intermediate.

SUITABLE MUSIC

For professionals, *anything other than* "Vogue" by Madonna, particularly early house, hip-hop, electro, and so on. For amateurs, *nothing but* "Vogue" by Madonna.

ETHOS

To Vogue well is to become glamor, become a facade, twisting reality for your own ends. As you sashay down the dance floor/catwalk, your mission is to become a different person—be that a straight Wall Street executive or an Amazonian model. The emphasis is on angular, linear, rigid, model-like moves smoothly connected to each other.

STEP 1

Bring your left arm straight ahead, palm out, then bring your right arm out to join it.

STEP 2

Cross your left hand so it rests above your right elbow, then cross your right hand over your left arm.

STEP 3

Lift your left hand up so the left arm forms a right angle, and repeat the move with your right arm so both hands are pointing up.

STEP 4

Lift both hands up above your head, then bring them down onto your skull, crossing over as shown.

STEP 5

Slide both hands around the back of your head, then push them both out at shoulder height so your body forms a "T."

STEP 6

Arc your right and left arms behind you in different directions (like you're tracing an invisible circle).

STEP 7

Then repeat Step 6, but form the circle in opposite directions.

STEP 8

Finish the move with the classic Madonna Vogue sandwich—left and right hands are the bread, your face is the filling.

The Kid 'N Play
(a.k.a. The Kick Step)

INSPIRATION
Kid 'N Play were a hip-hop and comedy duo, hailing from New York, who were hugely popular in the late 1980s and early 1990s. Unlike a lot of more recent rappers, they didn't swear, profess to being pimps, or go around pulling on their genitals. Nice boys they were, with their own cartoon show and series of films. And out of this multimedia extravaganza came the Kick Step, or as it soon became known, the Kid 'N Play, which has some similarities to moves such as the Roger Rabbit (pages 44–5) and the Running Man (pages 48–9).

LEVEL
Basic.

SUITABLE MUSIC
Early hip-hop.

SUITABLE PROPS
Wayfarers, high-top fade.

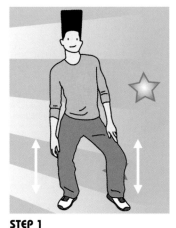

STEP 1
Start with your knees and feet far apart, bouncing twice on the right, twice on the left.

STEP 2
Hop onto your left foot and bring your right knee up to about waist height for a beat, then back down.

Note
For the full K 'N P experience, this move is best performed with someone else, though you wouldn't look that bad doing it on your own.

STEP 3

A few more bounces, then hop onto your left foot again with your right knee raised.

STEP 4

You then swing your lower leg from side to side, enough to notice, but not enough to kick someone standing a bit too close.

STEP 5

If you're doing this with someone else, allow your feet to touch lightly as you both swing in and out.

STEP 6

Moving onto your right foot, swivel through 180 degrees, while at the same time rotating your left knee...

STEP 7

... so although you're facing the opposite direction, your foot's still in place (if dancing with a partner, you should still be able to touch).

STEP 8

While dancing this move, bend and stretch your arms down in time with your steps.

The Grapevine

INSPIRATION

Sometimes, you may not want to get too technical or fancy with your footwork. The Grapevine is perfect for such occasions. It features in ballroom, club, and folk dances, but common to them all is a simple side-step motion with a modest flourish of stepping over the support foot thrown in.

LEVEL

Basic.

SUITABLE MUSIC

It has to be "I Heard It Through the Grapevine." You can choose whether it's the Gladys Knight and the Pips version or the more successful Marvin Gaye release that featured in the famous Levi's ad.

Note

The Hustle on pages 58–9 shows you how to add a Rolling Grapevine into a larger routine, and earn yourself some extra flash points!

STEP 1
Take a short sideward step, then step across and in front with your other foot.

STEP 2
Another step to the side, then step across and behind with your other foot.

STEP 3
You can continue in the same direction, or break and head off in another.

STEP 4
Roll your Grapevine by simply stepping further over, turning your whole body.

The Lawnmower

INSPIRATION

A move that comes from the mime school of dance, the Lawnmower is particularly suited to outdoor functions in the summer. All you're doing is cutting the grass, but without the incessant, annoying drone of the mower engine.

LEVEL

Basic.

SUITABLE MUSIC

Something by Savage Garden, or even any kind of grassroots music.

STEP 1

Start the engine—bend down and yank the invisible starting cord in time with the rhythm of the music.

STEP 2

Stand with your hands out in front of you.

STEP 3

Alternate lifting your feet in time with the music, swaying your hips as you go.

STEP 4

Occasionally wipe your brow with one hand—mowing can be a sweaty business!

Note

Why not tag on the Sprinkler (page 60) to keep the garden theme going? The move also has strong similarities to the Shopping Cart (page 144).

The Moonwalk

INSPIRATION

Is there anyone out there who doesn't think about Michael Jackson when the Moonwalk is mentioned? As much as he popularized it, however, he was far from the move's inventor— evidence of similar steps dates back as far as 1932, courtesy of Cab "Minnie the Moocher" Calloway. History aside, it's certainly a tricky one to master, but once cracked, there'll be no looking back.

LEVEL

Intermediate/advanced.

ETHOS

The general idea behind the move is to look like you're moving forward while at the same time moving backward, hence the alternative name for it when it is incorporated into a Popping routine: the Backslide. For more on Popping, go to pages 114–15.

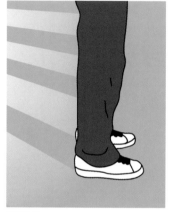

STEP 1
Start with both feet flat on the floor, about 6 in. (15 cm.) apart.

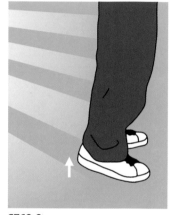

STEP 2
Lift up your right heel, keeping the rest of your foot on the floor.

Top Tip

Only try this on a flat, preferably polished surface wearing flat, grip-free shoes (or try just wearing your socks to start). Stilettos will make for more of a moon landing than a Moonwalk.

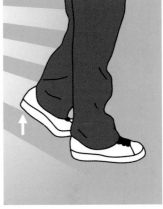

STEP 3
With your weight on the ball of your right foot, slide your left foot a little way behind your right.

STEP 4
As your left foot is sliding, slowly lower your right heel back to the floor.

STEP 5
Now for the other side: left heel up, weight on the ball of your left foot...

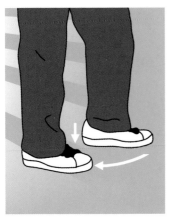

STEP 6
...and slide your right foot flat along the floor as you lower your left heel.

STEP 7
Once you're feeling comfortable with your footwork, try gently swinging your arms back and forth...

STEP 8
...as you effortlessly glide to give a greater impression of walking forward.

Climb the Ladder

INSPIRATION

A neat move that can easily be inserted into a more elaborate routine, or why not base your steps around this one? Climb up the ladder, climb down the ladder, put the ladder back in the garage. . . .

LEVEL

Basic—another move that can be performed sitting or standing.

SUGGESTED MUSIC

"Up on the Roof," "Ring My Bell."

STEP 1
Raise one hand a little above shoulder height and keep the other hand slightly below. Gently ball your fists.

STEP 2
Slide the upper hand down to below shoulder height and slide the lower hand above, both at the same time.

STEP 3
Slide your two hands back to the original starting points.

STEP 4
With accompanying enthusiastic lifts of the shoulders, repeat Steps 2 and 3 until you've climbed yourself out.

The Spin

INSPIRATION

A little move that should leave you feeling slightly exhilarated, if not dizzy, and your fellow dancers suitably impressed. The Spin, one of Michael Jackson's signature moves, and it can be a demon to master. For practicing, you need a fair bit of room, a flat surface, and some old socks.

Top Tip

Start slowly, and don't aim for too many rotations on your first attempts. Concussion isn't always pretty.

LEVEL
Intermediate.

SUITABLE MUSIC
Pop, RnB, funk.

STEP 1
Stand with your feet apart, your left slightly ahead and resting on the ball of your foot.

STEP 2
Swing your arms around your body a few times; this is essential for powering up the move.

STEP 3
Bring your right foot around, just onto the other side of your left foot, and rotate on your left.

STEP 4
Try and keep your momentum going by spinning 180 degrees on the ball of your left foot, then the other 180 on the heel.

Classic Moves

Pulp Fiction

INSPIRATION

A classic scene from a classic film. Mrs. Mia Wallace (Uma Thurman) has been taken out to a Hollywood-themed diner by one of her husband's associates, Vincent Vega—as played by John Travolta. A dancing trophy is up for grabs and the couple take to the floor in an attempt to bag it—Thurman particularly fortified by a prior trip to the ladies' room. You never actually see Wallace and Vega winning the competition, but the gong appears later in her apartment, leading to some speculation among Tarantino fans that they in fact stole it from the organizers. **The Best Dance Moves in the World. . . Ever** *in no way condones such dishonesty.*

LEVEL
Basic.

THE SONG
"You Never Can Tell," sung by Chuck Berry, was originally released in 1964 when it didn't greatly trouble the charts, though its use in Tarantino's 1994 film led to something of a resurgence in popularity.

Note

Wallace and Vega's dance is a fine example of how a series of apparently unrelated moves can be joined together to create a dazzling display. Most of the moves are featured elsewhere in the book, but the main jive is the Twist (pages 56–7). Take inspiration from Pulp Fiction *and make up your own!*

STEP 1

Twist for the first verse and chorus (see pages 56–7)...

STEP 2

... though add your own twists on the Twist (keep one foot flat, for example).

STEP 3

Shuffle back. Keep your right arm raised behind you while circling your left arm out in front of you.

STEP 4

Shuffle forward. Keep your hands by your sides but vigorously shift your shoulders back and forth.

STEP 5

Abbreviate the Swim (pages 30–1) with just a few front crawl steps...

STEP 6

... followed by a dive to the floor.

STEP 7

Then a few V-Signs (page 54)...

STEP 8

... followed by some Power Milking (page 164). Ad lib more Twisting, Swimming, and V-Signing until the music fades.

The Ska

INSPIRATION

Ska music originated in Jamaica in the 1950s and 1960s, and was a particular Caribbean fusion of jazz, calypso, mento, and RnB. Further punk flavors were added as it spread to the late 1970s U.K. and 1990s America. Characterized by an emphasis on the offbeat, a scratchy tempo, a walking bassline, and some juicy horns, much was made of ska's universal appeal, especially in its later incarnations—this was music for everyone to enjoy.

LEVEL

Basic.

STEP 1

Bow (but not too far) on the beat by bending your body forward from the hips, with your knees slightly bent.

STEP 2

Extend your arms out to the side on the first bow...

Note

These moves, and others like them, emerged out of ska's first wave, and they echo dances busted to other kinds of music popular at the time. These are a few basic steps, but there are plenty more where they came from!

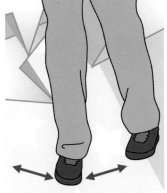

STEP 3

. . . and cross them over on the second. That's your basic ska step—just keep bowing and swinging.

STEP 4

Move your feet out and in on each beat, to add a little excitement.

STEP 5

Alternate your arm swings.

STEP 6

Extend both arms out in front, and take a step back.

STEP 7

Bring both arms back in as your other foot gets a look in. . .

STEP 8

. . . followed by a butt-push, and a straightening of the arms.

Rave On

INSPIRATION

Having taken a grip on the subway in New York and Chicago in the 1980s, house music crossed the Atlantic and gave birth to the U.K. rave scene, where thousands of people would gather in disused spaces, set up a music system, and dance until someone (usually the police) made them stop. Acid house was a variation of the music, and was characterized by squelchy synthesizers and distorted modulations.

Whether the name referred to LSD or the music's ability to burn holes in the dance floor is still open to debate. What's undeniable was acid house's power to create the last great youth movement of the 20th century.

LEVEL

Basic.

SUGGESTED PROPS

Baggy tee shirt, glo-sticks, whistle, beanie hat, smiley face badge.

STEP 1

Start with a gentle stomp—lift your feet up and down in time with the music.

Note

These moves are not fixed. Raves were open to anyone and the dancing followed that ethos. That said, certain moves emerged (indeed, some led to parody—see Big Fish, Little Fish, Cardboard Box on page 55)!

STEP 5

If the music becomes more "noodly," why not try and trace the notes out in front of you with your fingers?

STEP 2

Raise one arm up as the volume or musical intensity increases. You may like to shout something.

STEP 3

Swing your body from side to side, and maintain a wide grin on your face.

STEP 4

Raise up both arms.

STEP 6

Throw in a Big Fish, Little Fish for good measure.

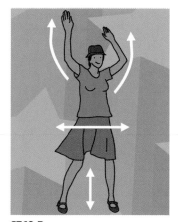

STEP 7

Raise up both arms, stomp your feet, swing your body from side to side.

STEP 8

Work your way around the whole dance floor, hugging strangers and telling them how much you love them.

Paint the Rainbow

INSPIRATION

Take two beautiful things—dancing and rainbows—and combine them to form a technicolored delight. Red, orange, yellow, green, blue, indigo, and, hey, don't forget the violet. Like Sunrise Sunset on page 86, this dance will also give your arms a pretty good workout.

LEVEL

Basic.

STEP 1
Imagine a rainbow arcing overhead and bring both arms up to touch its middle.

STEP 2
With your right arm, follow the rainbow's right side down.

STEP 3
Then do the same with your left arm on the left side.

STEP 4
Bring up both arms back to the starting position and start again.

Stack the Shelves

INSPIRATION

Ever been trundling around a supermarket and seen one of the employees stacking the shelves in an ugly way? Maybe the cans are misaligned, or maybe the labels do not face out. Right such retail wrongs by stacking your own shelves properly.

LEVEL
Basic.

SUGGESTED MUSIC
"Super(market) Trouper" by ABBA, "Aisle Be There" by the Jackson 5.

STEP 1
Turn right and place an imaginary can onto its imaginary shelf.

STEP 2
Turn left and repeat the can action.

STEP 3
Once mastered, why not move onto bigger items...

STEP 4
...placed on shelving at different heights? Enliven with shoulder twists and foot stomps.

Riverdance

INSPIRATION

Ah, Riverdance! Where would we be without Michael Flatley and his clog-wielding pals, jumping around and tearing up the linoleum? Based on traditional Irish step dancing, whereby the upper body remains stiff while the feet move with lightning speed and precision, the Riverdance first appeared during the interval of the Eurovision Song Contest in 1994. Demand since has been so great that it has become a global phenomenon, with shows selling out as fast as its dancers' feet fly.

LEVEL

Basic/intermediate, though watch the professionals and they redefine the term "advanced."

SUITABLE MUSIC

Emo, grunge, punk (joke).

SUITABLE PROPS

Anything green, clogs.

ETHOS

The coordinated stamp of feet on floor is the basis of any successful Riverdance. Intricate rhythms are beaten out en masse, making for some highly impressive dances. Beginners should aim to stamp in time with the music playing, but following too frantic a beat may well result in ankle dislocation for the unfortunate and over-ambitious first-timer.

STEP 1
Stand perfectly upright, back super-straight and with your arms down at your side.

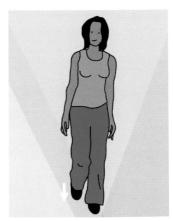

STEP 5
... followed by a stamp with your right foot, but this time slightly behind.

STEP 2
Hop onto your left foot...

STEP 3
...then stamp your right foot down slightly in front of you.

STEP 4
Hop back onto your left foot...

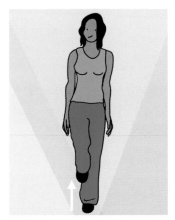

STEP 6
Hop onto your left again...

STEP 7
...and this time bring your right knee up and shake your lower right leg from one side to the other.

STEP 8
Beats can be emphasized by harder stamping.

Sunrise Sunset

INSPIRATION
This is a good move if you ever need to rejuvenate yourself mid-routine. Throw in a Sunrise Sunset, stretch your arms, breathe in deep, and you'll feel like a new dancer in no time.

LEVEL
Basic.

SUITABLE MUSIC
"Sunrise" by Norah Jones, or adapt it to the Jackson 5 hit "Blame It on the Boogie."

STEP 1
Standing with your feet roughly shoulder width apart, cross your arms straight down in front of you.

STEP 2
Arc your left arm counterclockwise and your right arm clockwise at the same time, keeping them nice and straight (Sunrise).

STEP 3
Arc both arms back to their original starting points, going in the opposite directions (Sunset).

STEP 4
Repeat, swaying hips and shaking head.

Note

Check out Paint the Rainbow on page 82 for a similar move you could also incorporate.

The Eggbeater

INSPIRATION
A classic nifty disco move, the Eggbeater features in the Hustle on pages 58–9. It can of course be used on its own or as part of any number of other routines. This move is not strictly about miming out the act of beating an egg—more a physical representation of how that egg must feel being beaten.

LEVEL
Basic.

SUITABLE MUSIC
Disco, pop.

STEP 1
Raise your hands to chest height, right in front of left, and gently clench your fists, facing toward you.

STEP 2
Vigorously rotate your fists around each other.

STEP 3
Then vigorously rotate your fists back the other way.

STEP 4
Pair this up with a simple foot move like the Grapevine (page 70) to add interest.

Classic Moves

The Conga

INSPIRATION

The perfect way to enliven any gathering, the Conga came out of Latin carnival traditions in the 1930s and 1940s. A dance that can only be performed with two or more people (preferably many, many more), it requires little know-how or dexterity beyond being able to move forward and kick out one leg to the side. Dancers should form themselves into a long line or train and follow each other around until the music stops. It's ideal for all ages, abilities, and body types.

LEVEL
Basic.

REALITY BITES

Technically, each dancer is supposed to guide the person in front by placing their hands on their hips and gently swaying them from side to side as the train moves forward. However, this rarely proves to be the case, particularly in non-Latin environments whereby any slinky sensuousness is replaced by an alcohol-fueled line barging around the dance floor, your auntie gets pushed into the punch bowl, and everyone collapses in a heap next to the brandy snaps. Come back Desi, all is forgiven. . . .

Note

Cuban musician and actor Desi Arnaz is said to have introduced America to the Conga with his Latin musical group in the 1930s.

STEP 1
Stand behind the person in front of you and place your hands on their hips.

STEP 2
Move forward for three steps...

STEP 3
...then kick out your right foot.

STEP 4
Move forward for another three steps...

STEP 5
...and kick out with your left foot.

STEP 6
Your hands should remain on the hips of the person in front at all times...

STEP 7
...and when it comes to the kick out, gently sway their hips in the right direction.

STEP 8
Keep going until the music stops or an accident happens.

One from Here, One from There

INSPIRATION

Choices, choices: where would the world be without choices? This move shows you can have all you want—just reach out and take it, greedy guts.

LEVEL

Basic.

STEP 1

With your right arm, reach across your body to the left side, then bring your arm back in.

STEP 2

Repeat the move with your left arm, stretching over to your right then back.

STEP 3

Alter the heights to which you reach—go higher and lower.

STEP 4

All the while keep your legs moving— right out then in, left out then in.

The Whip

INSPIRATION

This is a move particularly suited to the kinkier dancer, who may wish to throw a few subversive moves into their dance routine. Also suitable for those with an inner cowboy or cowgirl (in which case, you can pair it up with the Lasso on page 134).

LEVEL
Basic.

STEP 1
Raise your right arm above your head...

STEP 2
...and flick your wrist on the upbeat, as if whipping something or someone.

STEP 3
Practice the same move with your left arm—raise above your head...

STEP 4
...and flick, maybe more than once if you fancy. Move your hips as you whip.

The Baywatch

INSPIRATION

Scantily clad beach babes, hunks in trunks, and David Hasselhoff were the main ingredients in one of TV's most popular dramas ever. Set among the Los Angeles County Lifeguard fraternity, and featuring all the crazy adventures they got up to as they saved lives without sacrificing their hairdos, Baywatch caught the global imagination. Pull these moves and evoke the airbrushed perfection of an implausible sea rescue as performed by Pamela Anderson and Co.

LEVEL

Basic.

SUGGESTED MUSIC

Classic rock, soft rock, surf rock, rock on. . . .

SUGGESTED PROPS

Bikini/trunks, portable rescue buoy, whistle, an infeasible physique.

STEP 1

Start jogging on the spot, but in slow motion.

STEP 2

Stand still with your hands on your hips and toss your lustrous hair back.

STEP 3
Notice someone in trouble.
Point in their direction.

STEP 4
Run to help them, but in slow
motion.

STEP 5
Dive into the ocean: lift both
arms above your head, then
splash them down in front
of you.

STEP 6
Swim powerfully and
purposefully toward your
chosen target.

STEP 7
Rescue the victim and take
them back to shore.

STEP 8
Administer first aid, then run
back to the beach house (in
slow motion, of course).

The Travolta

INSPIRATION

Although disco originally started out as a predominantly gay and African-American phenomenon, Saturday Night Fever took the scene resolutely overground. Its star, John Travolta, soon proved to be everybody's favorite straight white disco dancer. This move has to be one of the most iconic to hit the dance floor. Strike this anywhere and people will immediately know what you're saying.

LEVEL

Basic.

SEE ALSO

It's used as part of the Hustle, featured on pages 58–9, and, of course, Saturday Night Fever on pages 24–5. Such is its status, however, that it deserves a page of its own.

STEP 1
Place your feet a little more than shoulder width apart, pointing slightly to the right.

STEP 2
With your left arm away from your body, point skyward with your right hand.

STEP 3
Bring your right arm across your body and point down and left.

STEP 4
Repeat with your left arm—point straight up, then down and right. Your hips should move in time.

The Shoegazer

INSPIRATION
Named after a particularly British musical phenomenon from the early 1990s, this is a dance move for those who really cannot stand the idea of dance moves, or are simply too tired or wasted to do anything energetic. The music was characterized by heavy guitars, barely audible lyrics, and distortion. The name comes from the tendencies of bands playing it to hang their heads and look at their feet during gigs.

LEVEL
Basic.

SUITABLE MUSIC
Typical Shoegazer bands include Ride, Lush, Chapterhouse, and Slowdive.

STEP 1
Stand still, feet almost together.

STEP 2
Bow your head and let your hair fall around your face.

STEP 3
You may want to sway slightly from one side to the other.

STEP 4
You can also indulge in a spot of Air Guitar (page 40), but keep it minimal.

The Chicken Noodle Soup

INSPIRATION

The Chicken Noodle Soup was a dance craze that flickered into life on the streets of Harlem in 2006 and went on to take YouTube by storm, making it something of an Internet phenomenon. With the accompanying song by DJ Webstar and Young B (ft. the Voice of Harlem), videos of dancers doing the Soup were soon receiving enough hits online for its popularity to spread far beyond the neighborhood and beyond New York.

LEVEL

Basic/intermediate.

STEP 1

As you hear the words "let it rain," bring both hands from above your head down to chest height.

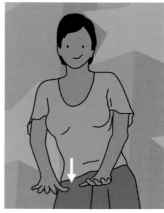

STEP 2

On "clear it out," lay your palms flat...

Note

The dance spawned some controversy: some posts online argued that the moves looked like those pulled in the early minstrel shows, while others just thought the whole dance supremely embarrassing....

STEP 3
. . . and move them in a horizontal circle in front of your body.

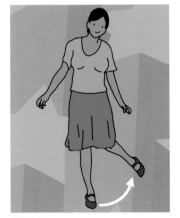

STEP 4
On "Chicken," hop onto your right leg and swing your left out to the side from the knee.

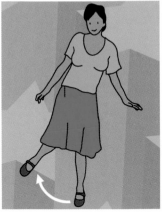

STEP 5
On "noodle," hop onto your left leg, swinging your right leg out.

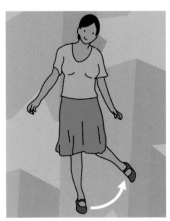

STEP 6
And on "soup," repeat Step 4.

STEP 7
You can also jump with both feet to the right on "Chicken" and "soup". . .

STEP 8
. . . and jump to the left on "noodle." Whatever does it for you.

Classic Moves

Y.M.C.A.

INSPIRATION

The sequence featured here, danced to the Village People's biggest hit "Y.M.C.A.," is a sure-fire winner for any dance floor celebration. It simply involves using the arms to spell out the four initials of the title in time with the chorus, and so can be enjoyed by anyone and everyone. Having started as an audience-rousing sequence for an American TV show on which the band were appearing, the routine has since become legendary.

LEVEL

Basic.

THE SONG

Take six young men from New York City and dress them up as a cowboy, an American Indian, a cop, a leather dude, a construction worker, and a member of the military. Give them some songs to sing about gay life in the 1970s and you've got yourself a band that will get even the most homophobic of grandmas up on the dance floor at any family party. As that brass riff intro kicks in, we all become Village People.

SUGGESTED PROPS

American Indian headdress, lasso, leather chaps, handlebar mustache, construction hat, and so on.

NOTES TO DANCERS

The dance routine is only strictly prescribed for the chorus, leaving dancers to express themselves more informally during the rest of the song. Beginners may like to simply sway, while a spot of interpretative dancing (rhythmically acting out the lyrics) is better suited to more advanced dancers. The first four steps featured here are only suggestions, while the last four should be busted by all concerned.

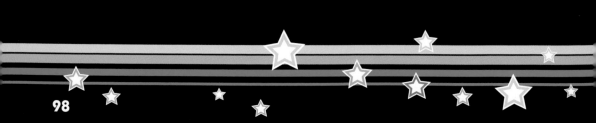

STEP 1
The military feel of the song can be echoed by marching in time with the music. Start on the spot, then try turning around or moving forward and backward.

STEP 2
When the phrase "young man" is said, point at a friend. If you don't know anyone, given the song's gay subtext, a safer option may be to point straight ahead.

STEP 3
Keep marching, and act out the lyrics; for example, "There's no need to feel down" can be a swipe of the hands and a shake of the head, then pointing down.

STEP 4
One favorite move for "ways to have a good time" is to thrust your pelvis backward and forward suggestively. Stay in time with the song, or you'll look too cheap and vulgar.

STEP 5
The chorus is the great unifier, when everyone comes together. As the band sing "Y," hold your arms outstretched above your head.

STEP 6
On the "M," place your left hand on your left shoulder, and your right hand on your right shoulder; or you can make an "M" in front of your chest. It's up to you.

STEP 7
For the "C," extend your right arm above your head and to the left, and your left above your waist and to your left.

STEP 8
On the "A," make a triangle with your hands above your head. Repeat the sequence three times, rotating your body 90 degrees, then return to the start.

The Cossack

INSPIRATION

The Cossacks are different communities of people based among the southern steppes of Ukraine and southern Russia. Their history is rich and varied, often colored by territorial disputes with larger, more powerful neighbors. These moves are just a taste of what is featured in their traditional dances and, when used correctly, certainly wouldn't look out of place on any Western dance floor.

LEVEL

Basic/intermediate.

SUGGESTED PROPS

Big furry hats, long colorful dresses, mustaches.

STEP 1

Jump forward onto your left leg, bending your right leg up toward your butt. Raise one arm.

STEP 2

Jump back onto your right foot, this time bending your left leg. Raise the other arm.

STEP 3
Repeat Steps 1 and 2 as you dance in a small circle. Watch out for other dancers.

STEP 4
Once the circle is complete, face forward, crossing your arms out in front of you.

STEP 5
Move your left leg out to the left, heel to the floor, and keep your right leg where it is, bearing your weight.

STEP 6
Jump and (quickly) change over: bring your left leg back in while straightening the right, heel to the floor.

STEP 7
Keep jumping and moving your legs in and out. Your weight will always be borne on the central axis.

STEP 8
The more adventurous may want to keep the movement going as you lower then raise your whole upper body.

Walk Like an Egyptian

INSPIRATION

*"All the old paintings on the tombs,
They do the sand dance don't you know."*
If you were born before 1980 you'll likely
recognize these opening lines from the
Bangles' 1986 chartbuster "Walk Like
an Egyptian." The song and its video
popularized this particular set of moves,
which echoes the depiction of figures as
they appeared in ancient Egyptian art:
angular arm gestures and two-dimensional
movements. It should be noted, however,
that ancient Egyptians did, in fact, walk just
like the rest of us.

LEVEL

Basic, though a wholly convincing Walk
requires some suppleness.

Note

*The angularity of limbs required to
successfully Walk Like an Egyptian has
affinities with certain hip-hop styles,
such as Popping, on pages 114–15. Once
you've got the Walk, why not try for a Pop?*

STEP 1
*Raise your left arm,
bending the elbow
with the palm face up.*

STEP 2
*Raise your right arm,
bending your elbow
with the palm down.*

STEP 3
*Shuffle sideways, and
move your forearms
left and right.*

STEP 4
*Accentuate this by
shifting your head
from side to side.*

The Q-Tip

INSPIRATION
Something nice and easy to throw into a larger routine. Personal hygiene should always be high on a dancer's list of priorities, so incorporating elements of your bathing ritual can make for fun on the dance floor (it can also be used with, for example, the Shower on pages 162–3).

LEVEL
Basic.

HEALTH WARNING
No matter how satisfying it is to dislodge a big wedge of earwax, hygienists advise not to insert cotton swabs too far into the ear canal, as it may compact whatever wax is already in there. Nothing to do with dancing, but worth saying nevertheless.

STEP 1
Lean out toward your left-hand side and raise your left hand to your ear as shown.

STEP 2
Twirl an imaginary Q-Tip in your ear for a count of four.

STEP 3
This time on the right—lean out, raise your right hand.

STEP 4
Twirl on for another four count.

Hammer Time

INSPIRATION
The gold sparkle shirt, the round glasses, and the unforgettable parachute pants. Stop, reader, it's Hammer Time. The biggest hit for Stanley Kirk Burrell, a.k.a. MC Hammer, was 1990's "U Can't Touch This," accompanied by a Day-Glo video featuring lots of bumping, popping, and this, one of his signature moves.

LEVEL
Intermediate—coordinating your feet can be tricky.

SUGGESTED PROPS
Parachute pants—if none are at hand, customize unwanted drapes.

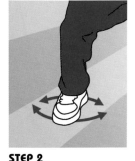

STEP 1
Stand with your feet a little more than shoulder width apart and pointing outward, with your knees bent.

STEP 2
To move right, swivel your right foot from the ankle, pointing to the right then the left at some speed.

STEP 3
Use your right foot as the engine, and slide your left foot along after it.

STEP 4
Then swap direction and power sideways with your left foot.

Top Tip

As with many similar foot-sliding moves, practice on a smooth floor with low-grip shoes or socks.

The Grind

INSPIRATION
It's inevitable that when bodies are moving to a particular rhythm, thoughts just might turn to pleasures of the flesh. Grinding can be done solo, but is more fun with two or more. If you are going to Grind in public, though, it's best to know exactly what you're doing—otherwise you'll end up looking a little sad and very sweaty.

LEVEL
Intermediate.

HEALTH WARNING
Sudden jerking of the head can trap nerves, or worse. Care should be taken at all times.

SUGGESTED MUSIC
Koochy RnB (fat basslines, crooned lyrics).

Top Tip

An Ass Shaker (page 26) can be incorporated, as can the Smooch (page 122), to lay it on really thick.

STEP 1
Stand with your feet slightly apart at first.

STEP 2
Working with the music, slowly gyrate your hips.

STEP 3
Continue gyrating as you grind your body up and down by bending your knees outward.

STEP 4
Touch yourself in appropriate places.

The Robot

INSPIRATION

The Robot had been around for a while, but it really came into its own in the late 1970s and early 1980s as part of the boom in hip-hop and electronica music. Man's love affair with the machine led to new noises and, inevitably, new moves. Whereas a lot of dancing is about cutting loose and shaking it out, the Robot is based on tight jerky movements, smooth transitions, and a high degree of control.

LEVEL

Moves get progressively harder to successfully bust.

SUITABLE MUSIC

Pioneers such as German electronic group Kraftwerk, hip-hop, electronica. Making machine-like noises with your mouth to accompany each move is also very much encouraged.

STEP 1
Stand with your feet shoulder width apart, your head up, chest and butt in.

STEP 2
Turn your head smoothly from side to side, as if it's being pulled by some invisible string.

Note

The Robot is a style of dancing, rather than a strict set of dos and don'ts. The key is to isolate each of your body parts and focus on them accordingly.

STEP 3
Lift your forearm up smoothly so your elbow forms a sharp right angle.

STEP 4
Lock your arm at the elbow, then rotate your shoulder through 90 degrees, then rotate it back.

STEP 5
Bend your upper torso (only) forward and back. Resist any temptation to groove anything below your waist.

STEP 6
To walk forward, slide your feet along the floor, keeping them as flat as possible.

STEP 7
Don't overstep, and stop each movement with a jerk.

STEP 8
To turn, simply rotate on your heel(s), keeping the rest of your body still.

Classic Moves

The Macarena

INSPIRATION

Sometimes, the stars align for a certain song with a certain dance, and out of nowhere word spreads all over the globe. Call it kismet, call it destiny, call it painful, but never underestimate the power of the dance craze. What started for an aging Spanish lounge act called Los del Rio as an impromptu party piece evolved into the worldwide phenomenon we know and love (or should that be "loathe"?) today.

LEVEL

Grandma-level basic. She may even know it better than you.

THE SONG

At a private party in Venezuela, Los del Rio (a duo who'd been together since the early 1960s) were performing their set when they noticed one particularly talented lady dancing in front of them. Improvising a chorus in honor of said dancer, the catchiness soon became apparent. Later that night, Los del Rio wrote the rest of what would prove to be their passport to riches, red carpets, and ridicule.

Note

These moves are for the refrain only; general jigging is appropriate for the rest. And while you are dancing, just lift your feet up and down in time with the music.

STEP 1
Lay your arms out in front of you, right then left, palms down.

STEP 2
Turn your arms over, right then left, facing your palms up.

STEP 3
Take your right hand onto your left shoulder, then left onto right shoulder.

STEP 4
Your right hand then goes behind your right ear, followed by your left hand behind your left ear.

STEP 5
Then your right hand down to your left hip, and your left onto your right hip.

STEP 6
And your right hand onto your right butt cheek, left onto left.

STEP 7
Saucy bit now—gyrate your hips around twice (any direction will do). . .

STEP 8
. . . and jump and turn through 90 degrees clockwise, clapping once as you go, and you're ready to start all over again.

The Harlem Shake

INSPIRATION

This move is closely related to the Chicken Noodle Soup (pages 96–7) and, as the name suggests, grew out of the same New York neighborhood. Legend goes that it started out as the Albee around 1981, as a drunken tribute to ancient Egyptian mummies who, because of their bandages, couldn't sit up properly; they could only shake.

LEVEL

Intermediate—it may take a while to master this move.

SUITABLE MUSIC

Hip-hop, RnB, anything vaguely jiggy.

STEP 1
With your feet around 12 in. (30 cm.) apart, arms by your sides, lift your right shoulder up toward your right ear...

STEP 2
...and push out your left hip.

Note

This move gets you emphasizing the beat by alternately pushing up your shoulders. It also allows for smaller beats with smaller shoulder push-ups between the bigger beats.

STEP 3
As you come back toward the center, slightly lift your left shoulder. . .

STEP 4
. . . quickly followed by your right shoulder (but not as high a lift as in Step 1).

STEP 5
Then jerk your left shoulder higher than before, push your right hip out, and hold it for a beat.

STEP 6
Then back the other way: two small, quicker shoulder shrugs followed by a big jerk on the right shoulder. . .

STEP 7
. . . and push your left hip out for a longer count.

STEP 8
Once mastered, bend your elbows slightly, keeping them by your sides.

The Mime Artist

INSPIRATION

Many of the moves in this book already have an element of mime to them—it certainly comes in handy when you're wanting to add a spot of interpretive dancing into your routine. Here, the classic Mime Artist move of being stuck inside a box is presented for your delight.

LEVEL
Basic.

SUITABLE MUSIC
"Living in a Box" by Living in a Box, "Trapped" by Colonel Abrams.

STEP 1
Lift up your right hand, palm flat and facing out.

STEP 2
Lift up your left hand so it's on the same horizontal plane as your right.

STEP 3
Move both hands around, ensuring they do not stray beyond the "wall," spoiling the illusion.

STEP 4
Turn to both your left and right sides, and then behind you, repeating these steps.

The Shimmy

INSPIRATION
The Shimmy's roots lie in Haitian voodoo dances, and it was made popular by African-American performers in the 1910s. However, only when it was performed by white dancers, such as Mae West and flapper Gilda Gray (the Shimmy Queen), in the 1920s did it really take a hold. It's an easy move, and shouldn't be confused with the belly-dance step of the same name. See also the Charleston on pages 168–9, another popular move from the time.

LEVEL
Basic.

HEALTH WARNING
Over-shimmying can cause neck and shoulder sprains: a slow build-up to greater speeds is advised.

STEP 1
Push your right shoulder forward and your left shoulder back...

STEP 2
...then swap over— left shoulder forward and right back.

STEP 3
Continue this motion while shaking your hips...

STEP 4
...and bending your elbows. The move can be danced quickly or slowly.

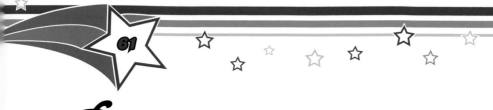

Popping (a.k.a. Hitting)

INSPIRATION

Popping (also known as hitting) is a dance that is based around the speedy contraction and relaxation of your muscles as you move, lending your body a jerking or jolting appearance. Such jerks are the "pops," which are then joined up with mimes and robotics to create longer rhythmic performances. It grew out of the street funk and electro scenes of the late 1970s and early 1980s and is still going strong.

LEVEL

Whatever level you want—real pros are up there.

SEE ALSO

The Robot (pages 106–7), the Armwave (pages 52–3), the Old Man (pages 166–7).

STEP 1
Raise your right arm out in front of you and contract and relax the muscles (the "pop") for a count of two.

STEP 2
Then raise your left arm and pop for two as well (these two steps alone form the "Fresno").

Note

You could fill a whole book solely with different popping moves: it's a wide ocean. What's here is a very basic introduction to a few popping moves, and throughout this book are other related steps you may want to try.

STEP 3
Raise and bend your right arm and pop for two...

STEP 4
...and do the same on the left side.

STEP 5
Extend your right arm out and bring it down to the left, bowing from the waist, and pop for two...

STEP 6
...at the same time, keeping your knee slightly bent and popping your thigh and butt muscles for a stronger hit.

STEP 7
Angles are very important, too—make sharp angles at your shoulders and elbows as you pop your arms...

STEP 8
...and sharp angles at your hips and knees as you pop your legs.

The Choo Choo

INSPIRATION
Whether you're doing the Loco-Motion or jumping aboard the last train to Clarksville or Trancentral, rail traffic has certainly played its part in the development of popular music. Honor the contribution with this tried and tested move.

SUITABLE MUSIC
"The Loco-Motion," either the Little Eva original or the later Kylie Minogue version.

LEVEL
Basic.

STEP 1
Bend both elbows, keeping your arms by your sides.

STEP 2
Extend both hands out and move them in a circular, forward motion (like the wheels of a train).

STEP 3
Bend your knees up and down in time with the music.

STEP 4
An occasional pull on an imaginary whistle with your left hand above your head won't hurt anyone.

The Corkscrew

INSPIRATION
Another example of how an everyday action can form the basis of something more extraordinary, and the simplicity of such mime-based moves makes them perfect for novices. Get comfortable with the action and you will soon find the beat.

LEVEL
Basic.

SUITABLE MUSIC
If only you could pull that cork out, you could read that "Message in a Bottle" by the Police.

STEP 1
Stand with your feet together, pointing out to the sides.

STEP 2
Bring your hands together in front of you at waist height, bending your elbows.

STEP 3
Bend slightly forward and pull your hands up and down (as if you're pulling up a corkscrew)...

STEP 4
...while bending your knees and moving your feet inward and outward in time with the hand pulls.

Classic Moves

The Chicken Dance

(a.k.a. The Birdie Song)

INSPIRATION

What family party would be complete without a rendition of the Chicken Dance, also known as the Birdie Song, Dance Little Bird, Fugladansinn, Il ballo del qua qua, Okashi Tori, or whatever you want to call it? The list of alternative translations for this oompah song points to how far its global spread has been since it was written back in the day. And where the song has been, its dinky little dance has followed.

LEVEL

Basic.

THE SONG

Swiss accordionist Werner Thomas composed the song in the 1950s, though it wasn't until the late 1970s that its appeal began to spread, first through Europe then further afield. Over 140 versions of it are in existence and a coop-shaking 40 million copies of them have been sold in total.

CHICKEN CONTROVERSY

There is a slightly different version of the one shown here. At Step 4, instead of wiggling your butt and arms, you can make a feathery tail with your hands behind you and then wiggle. Efforts to standardize the dance led to discussions at the United Nations, but in spite of the passing of various resolutions an underground resistance of "Tail-Shakers" continues to keep the variation alive.

STEP 1
Raise your hands to shoulder height and make beak shapes with your fingers.

STEP 2
Open and close your fingers for a count of four beats.

STEP 3
Then make wings by bending your elbows out at the side, and flap them for another count of four.

STEP 4
For the next four beats, wiggle your butt and arms down toward the floor...

STEP 5
...and, resuming your upright position, clap for the next four.

STEP 6
Repeat four times.

STEP 7
When the refrain changes, spin your partner around to the right for a count of eight...

STEP 8
...followed by a spin to the left for another eight. Then start all over again.

The Pizza Chef

INSPIRATION

Burn some calories while rooting your moves in the kitchen, miming actions that got you so fat in the first place! Instead of actually making a greasy pizza, just pretend while listening to some of your favorite music—the pounds will just fly off!

LEVEL

Basic.

SUITABLE MUSIC

Mozzarella Carey,
Gwen Stuffed-Crust-ani.

STEP 1
Make the base: knead the dough, pushing both hands down in front of you. . .

STEP 2
. . . then roll it out with an invisible rolling pin with smooth forward and back motions.

Note

The beauty of dancing the Pizza Chef is, of course, that you're not actually making a pizza. So moves can be repeated any number of times, the order can change, new ones can be added—reader, the choice is yours.

STEP 3
Chop some vegetables: using both left and right hands, one at a time. Chop with the beat.

STEP 4
Smear the tomato sauce: a smooth wrist action is integral to this move's success.

STEP 5
Decorate your pizza: drop the vegetables onto the base by alternately raising your arms and then releasing them from that height...

STEP 6
...then sprinkle some herbs over the finished piece...

STEP 7
...then slam it in the oven: use two hands on either side of your baking tray and slide it in as you bend forward.

STEP 8
Once ready, the pizza is ready to be sliced up with jazzy motions.

The Smooch

INSPIRATION
Relive the feelings of magic and wonder, probably originating in the schoolyard, when you first discovered that one could become two. This move could also work pretty well with the Grind (page 105).

LEVEL
Basic.

SUITABLE MUSIC
Plenty to choose from including "The Shoop Shoop Song (It's in His Kiss)" and "Kiss Kiss" sung by Stella Soleil in the United States and Holly Valance around the rest of the world.

   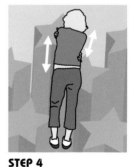

STEP 1
In time with the music, place your right hand on your left shoulder.

STEP 2
Then place your left hand on your right shoulder.

STEP 3
Gently sway your body up and down.

STEP 4
You may want to move your arms up and down too as you go, but be aware that you may earn unwanted cheese-factor points.

The Belly Roll

INSPIRATION
This is not a move you'll want to try if you've just eaten. One of the basic steps for belly dancers, the Belly Roll does take some practice to get the flow going, and works best for people with more muscle than flab in the gut region.

LEVEL
Intermediate.

SUITABLE MUSIC
Why not try the classic Beach Boys track "Gut Vibrations"? If that's not to your taste, then perhaps some RnB from the likes of R. Belly.

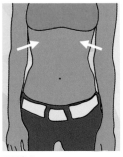

STEP 1
First, contract your stomach muscles, then slowly relax...

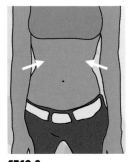

STEP 2
...then contract each region as you work your way down.

Note

The heavier dancer can try out the Truffle Shuffle, popularized by Chunk, a character in the 1985 film The Goonies. Simply lift up your shirt and expose your belly. Don't try rolling it; just wobble your flab around.

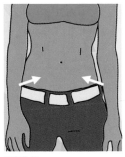

STEP 3
The intended look is one of a ripple flowing down through your belly...

STEP 4
...which can be heightened by adding in a hip grind or two.

The Six Step

(Downrock)

INSPIRATION

The Six Step is one of the fundamental moves of breaking/breakdancing/ B-boying/B-girling (the jury's still out on the most appropriate term to use). Breaking emerged at the same time as hip-hop, and dancers were able to focus on the new beat-driven music to power their moves. The Six Step is a classic example of the sub-genre known as "downrock"—all the action is down on the floor, where the emphasis is on nifty footwork and athletic acrobatics.

LEVEL

Intermediate/advanced.

HEALTH WARNING

This isn't a move for the elderly or those with weak arms. As with most dancing, but especially here, make sure you warm your body up a bit beforehand rather than jumping in cold.

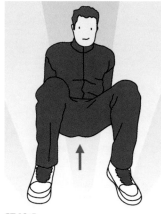

STEP 1
On the floor, sit with two hands behind you. Your knees should be bent out in front and your butt just off the floor.

STEP 2
Lift up your right arm and swing your right leg all the way around so the bend of your right knee rests up near your left ankle.

A Little History

Kool DJ Herc is the man most often credited with the rise of the breakbeat and hip-hop. By using two turntables, a mixer, and two of the same record, beats could be played and replayed; and dancers thrived on hearing extended percussive rhythms (known as "breaks").

STEP 3
Next, move your left leg straight out behind you (where it would be if you're about to do a push-up).

STEP 4
Then bring your right leg round and straight out, so you're now almost ready to do a push-up (with spread-out legs).

STEP 5
Now, take your right hand off the floor as your left leg comes through and your foot lands where your right hand was before.

STEP 6
Then bring your right leg around so the bend of the knee is just behind the bend of your left knee.

STEP 7
To finish, bring your left leg back to the starting position.

STEP 8
You may find it easier to use your fingertips instead of having your hands flat.

Classic Moves

The Hand Jive

INSPIRATION

Hand Jives are set sequences performed, as the name cunningly suggests, with the hands. Having gained popularity in the 1950s, particularly thanks to the Johnny Otis hit "Willie and the Hand Jive," the moves were often "danced" sitting down in theaters and around café jukeboxes. Twenty years later, the musical film **Grease** *featured a song, "Born to Hand Jive"; a whole new generation thus discovered the joys of dancing while sitting down.*

LEVEL

Basic—this move is perfect for the chair-bound or sufferers of the common complaint, two left feet.

SUITABLE MUSIC

Rock 'n' roll and early RnB. It's not very common to dance the Hand Jive to anything but those kinds of music, though you can always give it a go. You never know, it may suit Marilyn Manson.

TOGETHER IS BETTER

It is usual to dance the Hand Jive as part of a larger group, all doing the same actions at (hopefully) the same time. If there are detractors in your midst, however, don't force them into anything they don't want to, even if it's just a bit of thigh-slapping.

STEP 1
Clap both hands down twice onto your thighs.

STEP 2
Then clap your hands together in front of you for another count of two.

STEP 3
Lay your fingers out flat and shake your right hand over the left for another two.

STEP 4
Swap your hands over, left over right, and shake for two.

STEP 5
Make your hands into fists, thumbs facing up, and knock the right on top of the left for two.

STEP 6
Then knock the left fist onto the right for two more beats.

STEP 7
Finally, bend your right elbow, hold it with your left hand, and twirl your right hand through 360 degrees...

STEP 8
... then twirl your left hand, with your right hand holding your left elbow, for a final count of two.

The Bunny Hop

INSPIRATION

Depending where you are or where you're from, a bunny hop is a BMX bike jump, an ice-skating move, a computer or video game technique, or a rabbit on a trampoline. In the world of dance, there are two very different versions. The first was a form of the Conga (pages 88–9) from the 1950s, but it's the 2006 move, first made big by Luch Million$' rap song of the same name, that gets the attention here.

LEVEL

Basic.

SUITABLE MUSIC

Although this move is rooted in the Luch Million$ tune, you could incorporate it into any number of musical forms and songs, and it'll add a certain kick to your routine.

STEP 1
Stand on your left leg and raise your right knee out just in front of you.

STEP 2
Hop forward on your left leg, lowering and raising your right foot twice as you go.

STEP 3
Then repeat but on the other side.

STEP 4
The move should be smooth, with the front foot only just touching the floor. Lean back with elbows bent.

The Funky Chicken

INSPIRATION

It would appear that the humble chicken has had a noticeable effect on the world of dance. There's the Chicken Noodle Soup (pages 96–7), this Funky Chicken, and, lest we forget, the Chicken Dance (pages 118–19). Other yellow-feather-flavored dances are also available. Here, inspiration lies in the bird's unmistakable waddle of tiny legs, nearly buckling under the weight of a succulent, soon-to-be-devoured body.

LEVEL
Basic.

STEP 1
Stand with your legs together on the balls of your feet, and bend your knees out to the side.

STEP 2
In time with the music, keep bending your knees in and out so it looks like they're clapping.

STEP 3
While this is going on, alternately swing your arms out wide...

STEP 4
...then cross them over in front, right over left, then left over right.

The Indian Step

(Toprock)

INSPIRATION
Toprock is just as crucial when breaking as Downrock (pages 124–5), and the Indian Step (also called the Cross Step or Front Step) is one of the easiest to learn. Toprocking was arguably the first B-boy dance style, coming a couple of years before dancers started to get down on the floor pulling spins, rolls, and so on. As the name suggests, it's about moves to do when you're standing up, and introduces your audience to who you are and what to expect from your routine. First impressions count, so it's important to nail an impressive Toprock.

LEVEL
Basic/intermediate.

SUITABLE MUSIC
Good music to learn to is funk. Listen up for the snare (the 2 + 4 beats), and try and land your steps on it.

STEP 1
Stand with your feet about 8 in. (20 cm.) apart, with your hands together in front of your body.

Note
As steeped in hip-hop culture as it is, the Indian Step won't look out of place on any dance floor. It doesn't have to be limited to B-boy conventions, though purists may disagree. It's one of many Toprocks that can be combined with fancier moves.

STEP 5
And back, closing your arms.

STEP 2

Step with your left foot slightly in front of your right (toes pointing a little to the left) for a beat. Open your arms out.

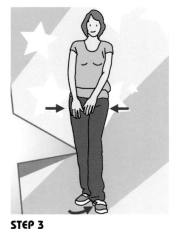

STEP 3

Start transferring your weight onto your right foot as you bring your left foot back, closing your arms as you go.

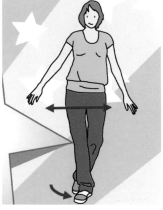

STEP 4

Now the right: step forward and in front of your left foot for a beat, arms open.

STEP 6

As you feel more comfortable, you can start taking larger strides...

STEP 7

... and make up things for your hands to do.

STEP 8

Remember to keep your head up too—it'll make you feel more confident.

The Worm

INSPIRATION
Although the Worm is most closely associated with breakdancing, and all that from the early 1980s, one of the first recorded Worms was performed by singer and comedian Sophie Tucker, otherwise known as the Last of the Red Hot Mamas, back in the day (the 1920s). The athleticism required, as well as its cute name, have conspired to produce a move with across-the-board appeal.

LEVEL
Advanced.

HEALTH WARNING
Ensure there are no sharp objects on the floor and that you're not wearing your best gear. It may sound lame, but protective pads may be a good idea for beginners, as your knees can take a pounding.

STEP 1
First, the stationary Worm: lie face down, head up, arms bent, and hands flat by your shoulders.

STEP 2
Push up your elbows, raising the whole of your upper body.

Alternative

Another Worm emerged during the punk era of the 1970s, whereby kids would just lie on their backs, shaking. It may not look as pretty as this one, but it's a lot easier to do.

STEP 3
Relax your elbows, and as your chest hits the floor...

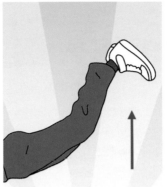

STEP 4
...kick up high. Push out with your knees, and follow off with your feet.

STEP 5
When your knees and feet come back down, that's the time to go for the next one: back to Step 2.

STEP 6
Now for the moving Worm: when you feel your chest meeting the floor, as you're kicking, slide your two hands slightly forward.

STEP 7
Then continue: lift up the top half of your body as your chest meets the floor...

STEP 8
...push out your knees then feet for a body-waving Worm.

The Lasso

INSPIRATION
The perfect move to saddle up with the Whip (page 91), the Lasso is also a rather adaptable dance move. Take the basic style and add or strip away as much as you feel comfortable with.

LEVEL
Basic.

SUITABLE MUSIC
Anything wild and west, such as the theme from *Rawhide*, or more recently Will Smith's "Wild Wild West."

STEP 1
Stand with one hand on your hip, feet about shoulder width apart.

STEP 2
Raise your other hand, bend the elbow, and start rotating your hand through 360 degrees.

STEP 3
As you feel more comfortable, you may want to raise your lasso higher (or lower)...

STEP 4
...and if you're really feeling it, try gyrating your hips as you rotate your hand.

The Wing Dance
(a.k.a. The Monkey or Knock Knees)

INSPIRATION
The Wing Dance, also known as the Monkey or Knock Knees, appears to have started out as a part of the Charleston (pages 168–9), but it warrants its own page here because it's a cracking little move that will delight and entertain both you and your fellow dancers. You should try to aim for a flow that will give the effect of your legs and arms blurring together.

LEVEL
Basic.

STEP 1
Bend forward, feet about 18 in. (45 cm.) apart, hands on your knees.

STEP 2
Bring your knees together, and as you do so, swap your hands over, so left onto right knee, right onto left knee.

STEP 3
Then bend your knees out to the side, keeping your hands in position so your arms cross.

STEP 4
Return your knees and hands back to the original position. Repeat until you fall over.

Note
Practice makes perfect with this move. Timing your knee bends with the music is a good idea, but the success of this move lies in speed, so up your tempo!

Classic Moves

Thriller

INSPIRATION

In late 1983, pop and plastic surgery phenomenon Michael Jackson released the track "Thriller," accompanied by a video directed by John "American Werewolf" Landis. Toward the end of the video, assorted zombies perform a routine including moves that have since passed into the Dance Hall of Fame. Perform any of them and everyone will know what you're referring to.

LEVEL

Basic.

THE SONG AND THE VIDEO

Such was the video's impact that it's hard to imagine the tune—produced by Quincy Jones and featuring a rap by actor Vincent Price—without it. The most expensive pop video to have been made at the time, it was a 14-minute mini-epic, based on the classic "boy meets girl, boy turns into a werewolf, girl wakes up" story. It also features cat monsters, the dancing dead, and a jacket with shoulder pads to make Sue Ellen Ewing weep.

Top Tip

Although the moves featured here form only a part of the full Thriller spectacle, ask yourself "How would I dance if I'd been buried for a few months?" Such a question should help you to style your routine.

STEP 1
Turn to the left, raising your hands in front of you like a begging zombie-dog. Stand on your left leg.

STEP 2
Now turn to the right. Keep your arms in the same position, but stand on your right leg.

STEP 3
Crouch down with both hands on your knees. Extend your left foot away from your body.

STEP 4
Rotate your body through 180 degrees using your right foot as a pivot. Keep your left foot out, dragging it as you turn.

STEP 5
Now shift your weight onto the left foot and turn 180 degrees the other way in a similar manner.

STEP 6
Keeping both hands on your knees, shuffle forward. Exaggerate with your shoulders.

STEP 7
Jump up to an upright position, and jerk your head sharply to the right, then the left.

STEP 8
Jerk your right shoulder up toward your ear, moving your head down to meet it.

Stir It Up

INSPIRATION
Another move inspired by daily events in the kitchen (see the Corkscrew on page 117 and the Pizza Chef on pages 120–1, for example). It's also closely related to the Cabbage Patch on page 33, but on a smaller scale.

LEVEL
Basic.

STEP 1
Stir the tea: hold an imaginary cup of tea with your left hand, palm up...

STEP 2
...then rotate your "spoon" clockwise and counterclockwise.

Note

Stir It Up has various levels from which dancers can choose. For daintier, prettier music, Steps 1–4 are recommended; otherwise, use Steps 5–8. You could also try incorporating the basic action into any number of larger or smaller vessels. It's Stir crazy!

STEP 3
Keep the movement going rhythmically and take your "cup" out to the left and right...

STEP 4
... and stir using your whole arm, not just your hand.

STEP 5
Stir the porridge: cup an imaginary bowl in the crook of your left elbow...

STEP 6
... and stir using your right fist, clockwise and counterclockwise.

STEP 7
Repeat on the other side.

STEP 8
Different consistencies will lead to slower or faster movements—decide which is best for the particular music.

Prince's Guitar

INSPIRATION
Call him Prince, Victor, Symbol, TAFKAP—the list goes on, as does his music. This move is taken from the video for his 2007 song "Guitar," where it's performed with jaw-dropping style and vigor by his two co-performers, the Twinz. It raises the game for air guitarists everywhere.

LEVEL
Intermediate—it requires a fair degree of flexibility. But it's worth it.

HEALTH WARNING
While Prince is a man who can look good in high heels, it's best to practice this move in flats.

STEP 1
Standing on your left foot, straighten your right leg up and across to the left...

STEP 2
...and hold it underneath with your left hand. Move your left hand up and down (like you're fingering a fretboard)...

STEP 3
...and strum/pluck the imaginary strings with your right hand across your upper right thigh.

STEP 4
Hop up and down on your left leg and shake your head to add a bit more wow factor (as if you needed any).

The Ickey Shuffle

INSPIRATION
Ickey Woods, fullback for the Cincinnati Bengals, pioneered this move as part of his (many) post-touchdown celebrations in the late 1980s, and it soon became part of NFL culture. So much so, in fact, that the league authorities slapped a ban on such performances a couple of years later. And once his footballing career was over, Woods used his Shuffle in a new job—selling steaks door-to-door.

LEVEL
Basic.

SUITABLE MUSIC
Anything victorious such as Collapsed Lung's "Eat My Goal."

Note
An alternative, more elaborate ending sees dancers raising their right hands, index fingers extended, tracing circles in the air, shouting "Woo Woo!"

STEP 1
With an imaginary ball in your right hand, step to the right, then left, then right.

STEP 2
Swap the ball to your left hand, then back again—step left, right, and left again.

STEP 3
Repeat Step 1.

STEP 4
Finally, three hops to the right and throw the "ball" to the ground (a spike).

The Skier

INSPIRATION

Sometimes, when it comes to dancing, you may not want to be moving all your body all the time, and with the Skier most of the action takes place above deck, as it were. It's a series of literal moves, inspired by the feeling of jumping and skiing up in the mountains. It should leave all dancers feeling alpine fresh.

LEVEL

Basic, though you'll need strong thigh muscles to keep it going.

SUITABLE MUSIC

Pop, rock, RnB (for example, "Snow Scrubs" by TLSki).

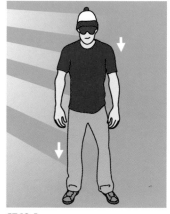

STEP 1

Stand with your feet about 12 in. (30 cm.) apart. Bend slightly forward and keep your knees bent.

STEP 2

Reach forward with both arms, keeping elbows bent.

Note

"The plow" is a term used by skiers for the position that slows them down as they come to a stop. It's therefore a perfect way to end your own ski-inspired routine.

STEP 3

On the beat, extend the arms, then bring them back to their original position, as if you're propelling yourself along.

STEP 4

You can choose to repeat Step 3 but by using alternate arms, instead of them both at the same time.

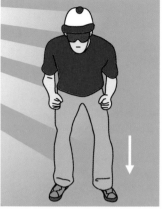

STEP 5

The Jump: crouch down further, then straighten your body at the same time as you lean forward slightly.

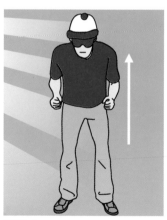

STEP 6

Maintain this position until either a) a big beat kicks in or b) you fall over.

STEP 7

Recover and continue skiing and jumping.

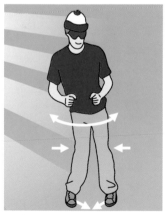

STEP 8

The Plow: bring your knees in slightly and then turn your feet slightly inward. Keep your hips moving.

The Shopping Cart

INSPIRATION
This move is pretty much a hybrid of the Lawnmower (page 71) and One from Here, One from There (page 90), and shares its environmental inspiration with Stack the Shelves (page 83). Which just goes to show that dance can be a marvelous melting pot where things cross over and interrelate. You could even try out the Lawnmower in a supermarket—how crazy is that?!

LEVEL
Basic.

SUITABLE MUSIC
That anthem of consumers everywhere, "Buy Buy Buy" by *NSync.

STEP 1
Bend your elbows and hold your hands in front of you, about shoulder width apart.

STEP 2
Reach out to your right side with your right hand...

STEP 3
...then stretch it out in front of you (as if you're depositing the item in your "cart").

STEP 4
Repeat Steps 2 and 3 with your left hand, then switch between left and right until your cart is full.

The Boxer

INSPIRATION
Commentators would often compare the elegance of a fighter like Muhammad Ali to that of a dancer, with his nifty footwork and agile grace. Forget the bloodied crunch of fist meeting flesh as two sweaty mountains of gristle attempt glory; concentrate instead on the fluid beauty of the prize boxer.

LEVEL
Basic.

HEALTH WARNING
Before performing these moves, ensure there's no one around within fist's reach.

SUITABLE MUSIC
Something fast like "Eye of the Tiger" by Survivor.

STEP 1
Standing about 12 in. (30 cm.) apart, lightly bounce on the balls of your feet and sway your hips.

STEP 2
Raise both arms with your fists clenched and (lightly) punch out twice with your right hand.

STEP 3
Jab out once with your left fist.

STEP 4
Continue with these and similar jabs, swaying and bouncing as you go.

Classic Moves

The Time Warp

INSPIRATION

The Time Warp features in the stage musical **The Rocky Horror Show,** *which went on to inspire the film* **The Rocky Horror Picture Show.** *Originally staged in 1973, the show continues to inspire something of a cult following in both its theatrical and cinematic incarnations. The Time Warp, originally conceived as a parody of popular songs with shouted-out dance moves as lyrics (the very idea!), has itself now become one such song. Que será será. . . .*

LEVEL
Basic.

THE SONG

The Time Warp serves as an introduction to the inhabitants of a ghoulish old mansion, discovered by the play's two ingénues, Brad and Janet, whose automobile has broken down nearby. Transvestites, goths, and other assorted freakoids take turns singing verses, with the whole ensemble coming together for "The Time Warp" chorus. Perhaps because of its easy-to-follow instructions, its popularity has reached a long way beyond its humble beginnings, and will doubtless get grandma on the dance floor at family occasions.

Note

These moves are for the chorus. Despite being called "The Time Warp," there is no prescribed action to accompany the line "Let's do the Time Warp again." So what you do is up to you!

STEP 1
Standing with your feet together, jump once to the left.

STEP 2
Then step to the right.

STEP 3
Then place both hands on your hips...

STEP 4
... and bring your knees in together.

STEP 5
Jump so that you're facing another dancer, then...

STEP 6
... execute one, or more, pelvic thrusts.

STEP 7
As the band sings "drive you insa-a-a-a-a-ane," gyrate your hips in a clockwise direction.

STEP 8
When it comes to "Let's do the Time Warp again," it's up to you....

The Pogo

INSPIRATION

The Pogo was the official dance of punk, a movement characterized by an almost moral disregard for square behavior. Punk came out of the United States and the United Kingdom as a reaction against what was seen as the watering down of the counterculture, spearheaded by 1970s bands such as MC5, the Stooges, and the Sex Pistols. It spat, it shouted, it couldn't play instruments, and the only dance it could muster was the Pogo, a taste of which is offered on these pages.

LEVEL

Basic.

Note

Pogoing may look dangerous from the outside—that was partly the point. It's a high-octane dance that can leave you bashed and bruised, but it's more about exhilaration than brutality. And it's a lot more fun with more than one.

STEP 1
Stand upright and stiffen your body with your arms by your sides.

STEP 5
Now start jumping around, straight up and down. . .

STEP 2
Stay rigid for a while, then start to shake a bit.

STEP 3
Start to jerk your head from side to side. Add a grimace.

STEP 4
Staying still, raise your arms from your sides to above your head and flail them around.

STEP 6
. . . or in any direction. . .

STEP 7
. . . adding a mid-air spin if you like.

STEP 8
Keep the anarchist spirit alive by throwing this book out the nearest window.

The Pop Princess

INSPIRATION

So full of pop they could have exploded from a blown piece of bubblegum, the Pop Princesses are just about teenaged and come with their own product lines of lipsticks, crop tops, lunch boxes, and lawnmowers. Their favorite color is pink, and record company execs love them. Feminists may regard them as post-millennial trailblazers. Like, whatever.

LEVEL
Basic.

SUITABLE MUSIC
Pussycat Dolls, JoJo, Christina, Britney, Whitney, Gene Pitney.

SUITABLE CLOTHING
Short skirt, low-cut top, school uniform, pigtails.

STEP 1
Start by swinging your hips from side to side.

STEP 2
On the beat, jump around to your right, raise your left shoulder up and down to the music...

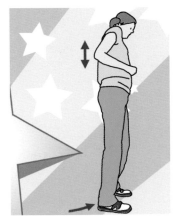

STEP 3
. . . then jump around to the left and raise your right shoulder for a few beats.

STEP 4
Jump back to where you started and run your hands down the sides of your body.

STEP 5
On a suitably strong beat, lift your right arm high above your head and to the right. . .

STEP 6
. . . and follow it with your left arm up and to the left.

STEP 7
Bring them down, crossing them over, so left hand is on right hip and right hand is on left. . .

STEP 8
. . . then lower and raise your body, rotating your hips as you go, lifting your shoulders up and down, and pouting.

The Mashed Potato

INSPIRATION

One of the classic moves of the 1960s, the Mashed Potato was ushered in first by Godfather of Soul James Brown, then taken further into the spotlight by Dee Dee Sharp's 1962 tune "Mashed Potato Time." Riding the same wave as the Twist (see pages 56–7), the Mashed Potato uses similar cigarette-grinding/potato-mashing footwork.

LEVEL

Basic, once you've worked out what goes where and when.

SUITABLE MUSIC

There's a whole host of 1960s tunes that are dedicated to the dance, including "Mashed Potato Twist," "Mashed Potato Party," "Instant Mashed Potato," and the revolting-sounding "Mashed Potato Jam."

STEP 1
Start with your heels together, toes pointing out.

STEP 2
With the weight on your left leg, lift your right heel and swivel out a quarter-turn on the ball of your foot...

STEP 3
... then take it back in.

STEP 4
On the next beat, lift your left heel and swivel it out a quarter-turn, before bringing it back in. Repeat as necessary.

The Monkey

INSPIRATION
Another move that burst out of the seemingly insatiable appetite for dance crazes to go with 1960s rock 'n' roll, though it's suitable for any number of other styles. For spreading a little jungle fever into your routine, go ape and do the Monkey!

LEVEL
Basic.

SUITABLE MUSIC
"The Monkees Theme," of course; but you don't have to keep it simian; any primate will do—you can even bop the Monkey to the Gorillaz if you want.

STEP 1
Lean slightly forward from your waist, both arms bent with your thumbs up.

STEP 2
Turn to the left, bend a bit lower, and raise your right thumb.

Style Tip
You are a monkey holding a banana in each hand.

STEP 3
On the next beat, return to your starting position. . .

STEP 4
. . . and on the next, turn to the right, bend lower, and raise your right thumb. Then repeat from Step 1.

Kung Fu Fighting

INSPIRATION
Demonstrating that inspiration can be found in the cheesiest of places, Kung Fu Fighting owes a debt of gratitude to the classic Karate Kid movies. The moves taught by Mr. Miyagi to his young protégé Daniel can be applied as equally to the dance floor as they are to the sports arena. And remember, in art, as in life: "breathe in through nose, out of mouth."

LEVEL
Basic.

SUITABLE MUSIC
"Kung Fu Fighting" by Carl Douglas, obviously.

POSITIONING
This move can be busted either standing up or, for the more supple, down on one knee.

STEP 1
Bow quickly and neatly with your feet together.

STEP 2
Wax on: bend your right elbow and rotate your palm, face out, through 360 degrees clockwise.

STEP 3
Wax off: bend your left elbow and rotate your palm through 360 degrees counterclockwise.

STEP 4
Paint the fence: hold an invisible paintbrush and glide it over an invisible fence in front of you, up and down in time with the music.

STEP 5
Catch the fly: make beak shapes with your hands (chopstick stand-ins) and snap them artfully.

STEP 6
Guard up: rock your body back and forth with your left arm bent close to your side, right arm bent in front of you.

STEP 7
Throw in a few karate chops to your left, right, and center.

STEP 8
The ending crane: hold your arms out above your head, standing on your left leg, right leg raised at 90 degrees.

The Cha-Cha Slide

INSPIRATION

Another song with the instructions for dancers shouted out by the MC (see also Time Warp on pages 146–7 and Agadoo on pages 34–5). It's nice and easy, your grandma will love it, and it'll get played at family parties and you'll wonder why you don't call them so often. Fat and thin, old and young, insane and sane: the Slide's for all.

LEVEL

Basic.

THE SONG

Originally recorded to accompany an aerobics class in 1996, the Cha-Cha Slide has gone on to inspire dancers and partygoers in both America and Europe. Its creator, DJ Casper (also known as Mr. C), has said, "If you do the dance properly, you feel it everywhere." You've been warned.

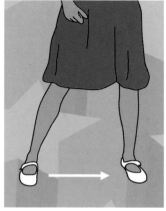

STEP 1
"To the left now": take two steps to the left.

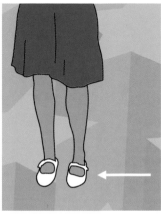

STEP 2
"Take it back now": two steps back, starting with the right foot.

Note

Space prevents a full breakdown here, but Mr. C's instructions are so clear that it's not so terribly hard to catch his drift once the song is playing. What is on these pages is a brief description of some of the more challenging moves in what is an essentially unchallenging routine.

STEP 3
"Now Cha Cha": right foot over left, then left back, then right to the right side, then left forward.

STEP 4
"Turn it out": step to the left, then turn 90 degrees to the left as you then step with your right foot.

STEP 5
"Kriss Kross": jump up feet apart, jump up legs crossed and repeat.

STEP 6
"Hands on your knees": see the Wing Dance on page 135.

STEP 7
"How low can you go?": work your body as near to the floor as your joints will allow.

STEP 8
"Reverse": try and spin 360 degrees in the air.

Greased Lightnin'

INSPIRATION

Ever loved an automobile so much you want to make a song and dance about it? That man again, Travolta, certainly did in the 1978 film **Grease***, and got his buddies to join in too. This signature move from their routine goes to show how much passion an engine on four wheels can inspire.*

LEVEL
Basic.

SUITABLE CLOTHING
Cap-sleeved T-shirt, pompadour haircut, white socks, artfully placed oil smudge on face.

STEP 1

Stretch your right arm out to the right, palm down, and glide it in an arc to the left.

STEP 2

Raise it straight up and down above your head...

STEP 3

... then stretch it straight out to the right, then straight back in.

STEP 4

Repeat Steps 2 and 3. Then mirror the whole move using your left arm.

The Stomp

INSPIRATION

The Stomp can be easily inserted into a general routine if you want to emphasize a particularly strong beat or series of beats. Stompers should always ensure that nothing or no one lies between their foot and the floor. If there is, it's not called dancing; that's violence.

LEVEL

Basic.

SUITABLE MUSIC

Disco, pop, funk, "Stomp!" by the Brothers Johnson (naturally).

STEP 1
Stand with your feet about 12 in. (30 cm.) apart.

STEP 2
On the beat, stamp your foot on the floor.

STEP 3
For variation, stomp in front of you, to the side, or behind...

STEP 4
...and use your other foot. Enliven your stomps with hip- and arm-swaying.

Napoleon Dynamite

INSPIRATION

If proof was ever needed of the power of a carefully crafted dance routine, here it lies. In the 2004 independent film **Napoleon Dynamite,** *the eponymous hero gives a performance in front of his fellow high-school students that leads to a standing ovation and the crowning of his friend Pedro as school president. Ugly duckling Napoleon is transformed into a white swan of grace, beauty, and downright funkability, firmly squishing the egos of his jock nemeses under his snazzy blue moon boots.*

LEVEL

Intermediate.

SUGGESTED CLOTHING

Perm, glasses, big teeth, "Vote for Pedro" slogan T-shirt, moon boots.

POSITIONING

This move can be busted either standing up or, for the more supple, down on one knee.

SUITABLE MUSIC

You can do this to masses of tunes, but Napoleon himself throws his shapes to "Canned Heat" by Jamiroquai.

STEP 1

Walk backward, crouching down and lifting your knees higher than usual. Arms by your side.

STEP 5

. . . and raise your right hand above your head, swaying it from side to side as you go. Gyrate your hips.

Note

A number of moves in Napoleon's routine are featured elsewhere in this book. Here are some that got away. . . .

STEP 2
Raise your right arm and angle your hand to the right, then side-step to the left for four...

STEP 3
... then quickly turn left; clap your hands, keeping your elbows in at your side, and flick back your hair.

STEP 4
Legs far apart, knees bent, left hand on left hip, and face to the left...

STEP 6
Hold your left hand, palm up, at chest height, and bring your right hand over in an arc and clap it.

STEP 7
If there's room, gambol forward on the floor...

STEP 8
... and finish by bringing out your left hand and pointing straight ahead.

The Shower

INSPIRATION

While it may be perfectly acceptable to sing and dance in the shower, have you ever tried showering on the dance floor? It's always a good idea to have a wash before you bust (too much of your funk will soon leave you dancing solo), and this sequence relives those essential components of a good rub 'n' scrub.

LEVEL

Intermediate.

SUITABLE MUSIC

Pop, RnB, Loofah Vandross.

ADVICE

Keep your clothes on—you're only pretending!

STEP 1
Stand with your left arm at your side and bring your right arm up to chest height, reaching to the left, palm out.

STEP 2
Slide your right arm across your body to open the shower door (or curtain if you prefer).

STEP 3

Step into the shower using an exaggerated swagger (which foot goes first is not important at this stage). Close the door or curtain behind you.

STEP 4

Turn to face the shower unit, reach out with your right arm, and turn your hand clockwise to start the water.

STEP 5

Feel the water pouring over you. Are you using a sponge or flannel? Is the water hot or cold? All require appropriate moves and help personalize your routine.

STEP 6

Turn off the shower.

STEP 7

Reopen the door/curtain, swagger back out, close the door/curtain.

STEP 8

The final rubdown. Grab both ends of an imaginary towel and, with the left arm in front and the right arm behind, dry between your legs.

Power Milking

INSPIRATION

A recognizable move first seen around the 1950s and 1960s, Power Milking is still enjoyed around the globe of dance. Imagine you are a milkmaid confronted with udders so huge that, if you slack off in your job, the poor beast in front of you will explode: not a good look.

LEVEL
Basic.

SUITABLE MUSIC
Rock 'n' roll, pop (for example, "Cow Will I Know" by Whitney Moo-ston, and so on).

STEP 1
Turn your body to the right, clench your fists (lightly), and bend your arms, with your right hand higher than the left.

STEP 2
On the beat, bring your left hand up and your right hand down. Continue for four beats.

STEP 3
Then turn to the left and repeat the hand action.

STEP 4
Continue in this vein, pulling those "udders." Try nodding your head as you Milk, and maybe add some fancy footwork.

Hail to the King

INSPIRATION
Probably not the best move if you're dancing with a) someone whose heart you are seeking to win or b) your uncle. A pelvic thrust by any other name, Hail to the King is something of a classic, and is inspired by the original gyrator, Elvis. Indeed, his rotations once flustered so many TV viewers (800,000 wrote to the station to complain) that his future performances were shot from the waist up only.

LEVEL
Basic.

HEALTH WARNING
Too much of a thrust could lead to groin strain, even a hernia; seek medical advice before attempting if you are concerned.

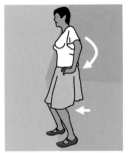

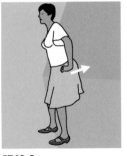

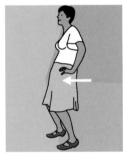

STEP 1
Stand with your feet far apart, knees bent. Bend your arms and place your hands on your hips.

STEP 2
Push out your butt...

STEP 3
... then, on the beat, push your hips forward (forcefully, if the mood takes you).

STEP 4
Jump forward on each thrust, reaching forward then back as if using your hips to propel you forward.

The Old Man

INSPIRATION

This is another move related to Popping (pages 114–15) and is part of a style known as electric boogaloo, or just boogaloo for short. The Electric Boogaloos were a street dance band from California who pioneered both dances in the late 1970s (though this is hotly contested). Whereas Popping concentrates on moves that are based on muscle contraction, Boogaloo focuses on fluid movements, especially of the lower body. The Old Man is a good example of this.

LEVEL

Intermediate.

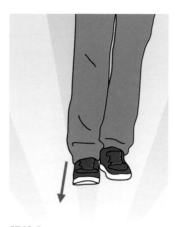

STEP 1

Stand with both feet together, then swing your right foot out in front of you. . .

STEP 2

. . . so your heel gently brushes the floor, then bring it out to the right side and down.

Note

This move can be easily tagged onto the Fresno (the first two steps of the Popping moves on page 114–15) to spin your routine out a little longer.

STEP 3

As your foot hits the floor, lift up your left shoulder so there's an invisible line running from there to your right foot.

STEP 4

Then move your left shoulder down and your right shoulder up as your upper body glides over to the right.

STEP 5

Step to the middle with your left foot. . .

STEP 6

. . . then swing out your right foot, as in Step 1. . .

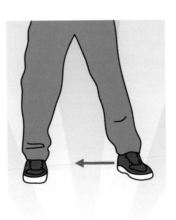

STEP 7

. . . step to the middle again with your left, as in Step 5. . .

STEP 8

. . . then you're free to either start all over again or pop some new steps for variation.

The Charleston

INSPIRATION

Throughout history, certain dances become forever associated with particular social or political movements (for example, the Twist on pages 56–7 and Vogue on pages 66–7). The Charleston is one such dance, and while the music it was originally performed to may sound outdated on the modern dance floor, the moves themselves are still fit to bust.

LEVEL

Intermediate.

HISTORY

Much like the Shimmy (page 113), the Charleston grew out of African dance traditions, but it only got properly popular in the 1920s, once the white folks were doing it, too. At the time it was seen as immoral and corrupt (similar to initial takes on the U.K. rave scene of the late 1980s), a dance that the "dry" people would never indulge in (this was, of course, the time of Prohibition). Now we're all a lot "wetter," and the Charleston has mutated into many forms—the most basic steps are featured here.

SUITABLE MUSIC

Something fast and furious like "Doop" by Doop.

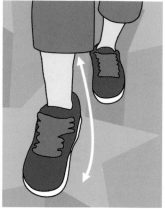

STEP 1
Walk one step forward, then one step back with your right leg. . .

STEP 5
Twist in and out on the ball of your left foot.

Note

Another move you may want to chuck into your Charleston is the Wing Dance, featured on page 135.

STEP 2
. . . then one step backward and another forward with your left leg.

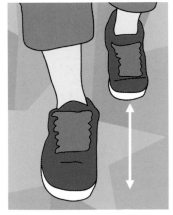

STEP 3
Flap your arms around as you go (hence the term "flapper") and add a bounce to each step.

STEP 4
Now put your heels together, both feet facing out.

STEP 6
Extend both arms as you swing your right foot out and forward for a beat.

STEP 7
Bring everything back in, twisting again on your left foot, landing in Step 4 position. Change over, so twist on your right foot. . .

STEP 8
. . . while your left foot swings out and down.

The Watusi

INSPIRATION

Another move that heralded the birth of rock 'n' roll, the Watusi was nearly as popular as the Twist. It was unleashed in the early 1960s and even had its own song—"El Watusi" by the Puerto Rican jazz man Ray Barretto. Not to be confused with the watusi cow, whose horns have to be seen to be believed.

LEVEL

Basic.

SUITABLE MUSIC

Typically rock 'n' roll, or anything requiring a 1960s flavor.

STEP 1

Standing with your feet about 12 in. (30 cm.) apart, swing your hips to the right.

STEP 2

As you do so, bring both arms up to the right-hand side, about pelvis level.

STEP 3

Then swing your hips to the left...

STEP 4

...and your arms down and around in a semicircle. Keep on swinging from left to right.

The Scarecrow

INSPIRATION

If you're not too comfortable dancing with your hands by your side, why not stick them out at right angles to the rest of your body? The Scarecrow allows for such a distinctive formation, and should go some way to impressing fellow dancers on the floor. Essentially, you're dancing like you've got a broom wedged across your back and through your shirtsleeves.

LEVEL

Basic.

STEP 1
Relax both shoulders, standing with feet about 12 in. (30 cm.) apart.

STEP 2
Raise both arms out to the side so they're parallel with the floor.

STEP 3
Move your feet in a shuffling side-to-side motion.

STEP 4
Add variation to your routine by swaying your body from side to side, tipping your arms in alternate directions.

Note

The humble Scarecrow also influenced a style of street dance linked to Popping (see pages 114–15). It uses a similar kind of stance to the Scarecrow, but involves "popping" the arms and chest.

The Christmas Tree

INSPIRATION

The end of the book and the end of another year. Snow is falling, kids are singing carols, the store registers are in meltdown, and the suicide rate is rocketing. Ah yes, Christmas comes but once a year, and decorating the tree requires skill and dexterity. So what better activity to inspire this fine set of moves?

LEVEL

Basic.

SUGGESTED MUSIC

Carols and other assorted festive tunes.

STEP 1

Mime the basic tree shape: crouch down with your feet together, arms outstretched.

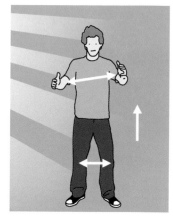

STEP 2

Rise up, bringing your knees and arms in and then out as you go.

STEP 3
The further you rise, the closer your arms and knees become. Until you reach the highest branch.

STEP 4
The tinsel: sway your hips as you bend your arms...

STEP 5
...then gracefully place the imaginary tinsel on the tree. Repeat a few times.

STEP 6
The jingle bells: bring each hand up to your ear in turn and shake an imaginary bell.

STEP 7
The lights: recreate the joys of tiny flashing lights by quickly opening and closing your fists.

STEP 8
The fairy: finally, reach up with your right arm, standing on one leg, and drop the fairy into place.

Index